Introducing Islamic Carpets

Noorah Al-Gailani

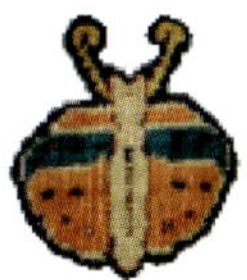

The Burrell
Collection

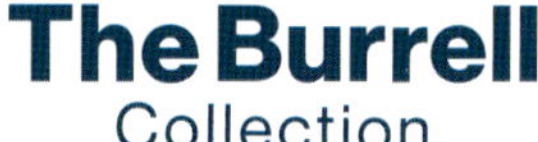

First published in 2022 by Glasgow Museums Publishing.
Text © Culture and Sport Glasgow (Museums) 2022.
Images © CSG CIC Glasgow Museums Collection, unless otherwise acknowledged.

ISBN 978-1-908638-38-0

Written by Dr Noorah Al-Gailani
Edited by Kim Teo
Designed by Jacqui Duffus
Photography by Enzo Di Cosmo and Iona Shepherd
Reprographic scanning by Alan Broadfoot and Iona Shepherd
Images supplied by Glasgow Museums Photo Library
www.csgimages.org.uk
www.glasgowmuseums.com

Front cover image: Carpet fragment with grotesque-animal design (detail), Safavid period, late 1500s–early 1600s, 9.23 (pp. 56–57)
Back cover image: Arabesque carpet fragment with cloud-band design, Safavid period, late 1500s–early 1600s, 9.11 (p. 36)
Title page image: Butterfly from the Wagner garden carpet, Safavid period, about 1600–1700, 9.2 (pp. 18–21).

Acknowledgements

We are very grateful to the textiles specialist Mrs Jennifer M Scarce for reviewing this book.

All efforts have been made to trace copyright holders, but if any omissions have been made inadvertently, please contact the publishers. We are very grateful to the following for permission to reproduce images: Alamy Stock Photo (p. 62, both images); Bodleian Libraries, University of Oxford (p. 57, right); Encyclopaedia Britannica, Inc. (p. 9, reprinted with permission from *Encyclopaedia Britannica*, © 2008); Hali Publications Ltd (p. 53, left); United States Library of Congress Prints and Photographs Division (p. 69).

Printed in Scotland by J Thomson Colour Printers, Glasgow
Cover printed on 350gsm Galerie Satin; text printed on 150gsm Galerie Satin

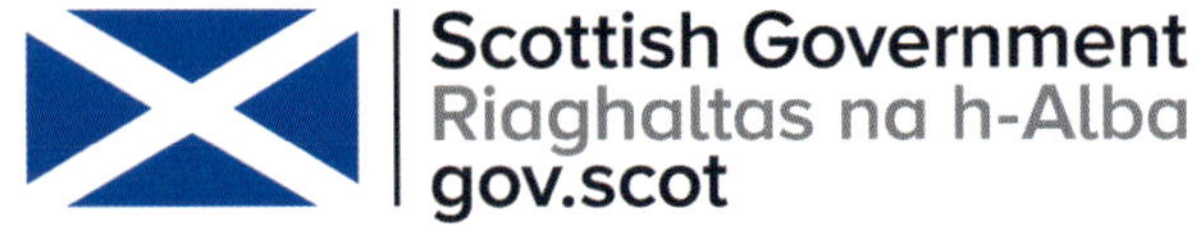

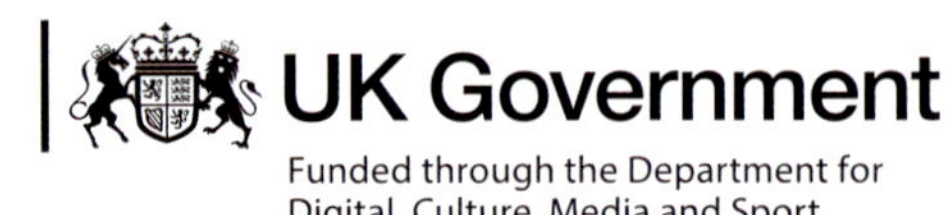

Contents

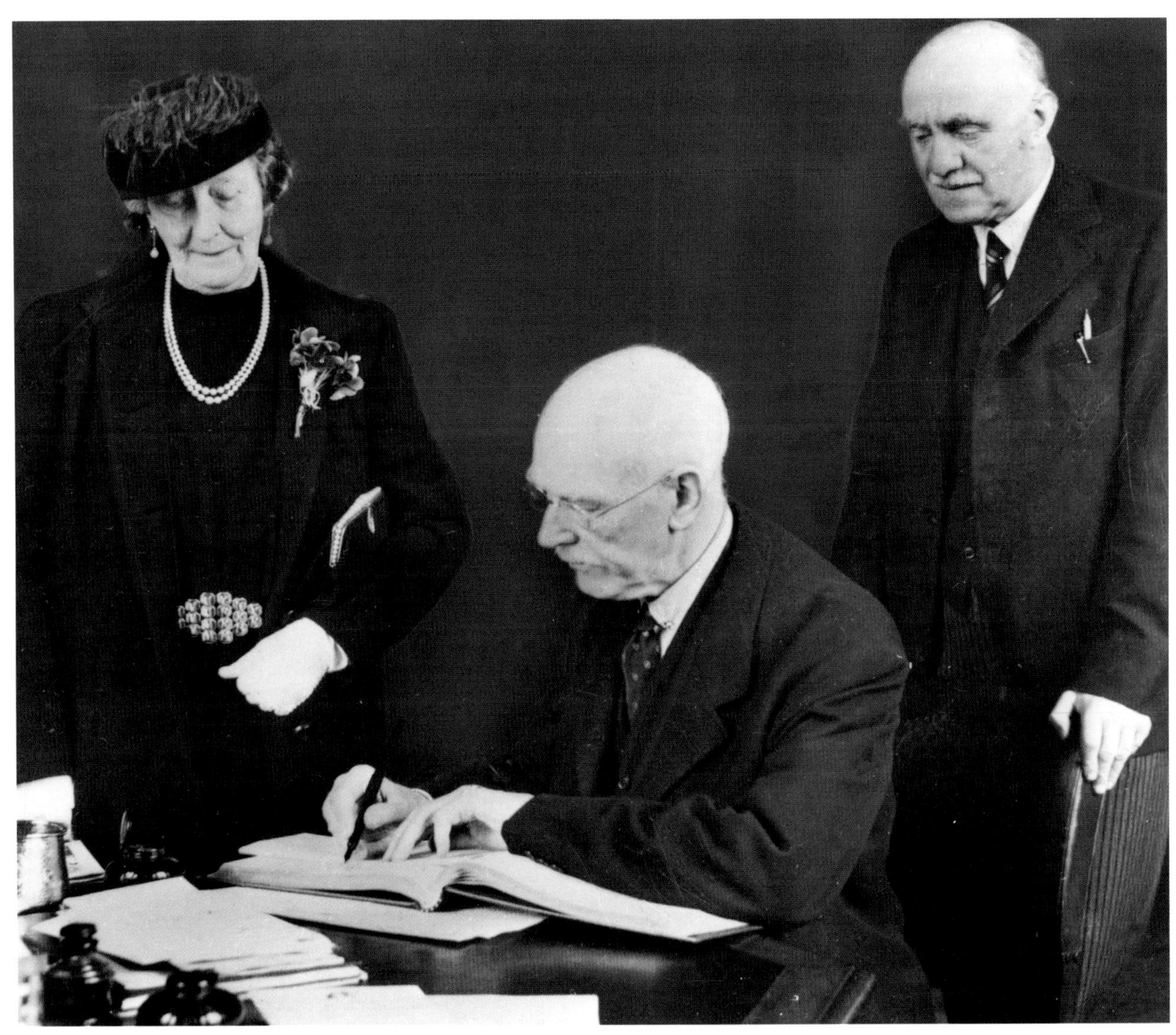

Sir William Burrell (seated), Constance, Lady Burrell and
Lord Provost James Welsh at the City Chambers, Glasgow,
1944, on the occasion of Sir William receiving the Freedom
of the City of Glasgow. Glasgow Museums Archive,
GMA.2013.1.1.470.

The Burrell Collection: The Gift of Sir William and Constance, Lady Burrell

The Burrell Collection comprises over 9,000 objects gifted to the city of Glasgow by Sir William Burrell (1861–1958) and his wife Constance, Lady Burrell (1875–1961). The main gift, of around 6,000 objects, was in 1944, but Burrell continued to add to it until his death, and the Collection has been further augmented with funds gifted by Burrell and administered by the Burrell Trustees.

Sir William made his fortune in shipping at a time when Glasgow was second city of the Empire. Collecting was a lifelong passion, and his treasures adorned his various homes: archive photographs show tapestries, sculpture, paintings and furniture in his house in Great Western Terrace, Glasgow. These, and also ceramics, stained glass, arms and armour, and carpets and other textiles, were displayed at Hutton Castle, his home in the Scottish Borders.

A sophisticated collector with a discerning eye, Burrell appreciated fine craftsmanship and meticulous attention to detail. From tapestries to sculpture, nineteenth-century French art to Chinese bronzes, medieval stained glass to Islamic carpets, the breadth and quality of his collection demonstrate his wide-ranging embrace of different cultures and art forms. Sir William also gave money for a new building to house his collection, and it is now displayed in a purpose-built museum in the centre of Pollok Country Park, on the south side of Glasgow. The park was gifted to the city in 1967 by Mrs Anne Maxwell Macdonald (1906–2011), and a competition, sponsored by the Royal Institute of British Architects, was held to design a suitable building within it to house the Collection. The winners of the competition, architects Barry Gasson, John Meunier and Brit Andresen, came up with a building which not only displays the Collection to advantage, but is also in harmony with the surrounding parkland. The building opened in 1983, but through the decades the Scottish weather took its toll and in 2016 the Category-A listed building closed for an ambitious programme of refurbishment, redisplay and reinterpretation.

This series is designed to introduce different parts of the Collection. Written by subject specialists, each book gives an insight into the Burrell's treasures. We, the Trustees of the Burrell Collection, are delighted to see the amount of new research that has been carried out on the objects in the Collection, and hope that visitors will continue to enjoy Sir William and Constance, Lady Burrell's gift for many generations to come.

Professor Frances Fowle
Senior Trustee, Sir William Burrell's Trust

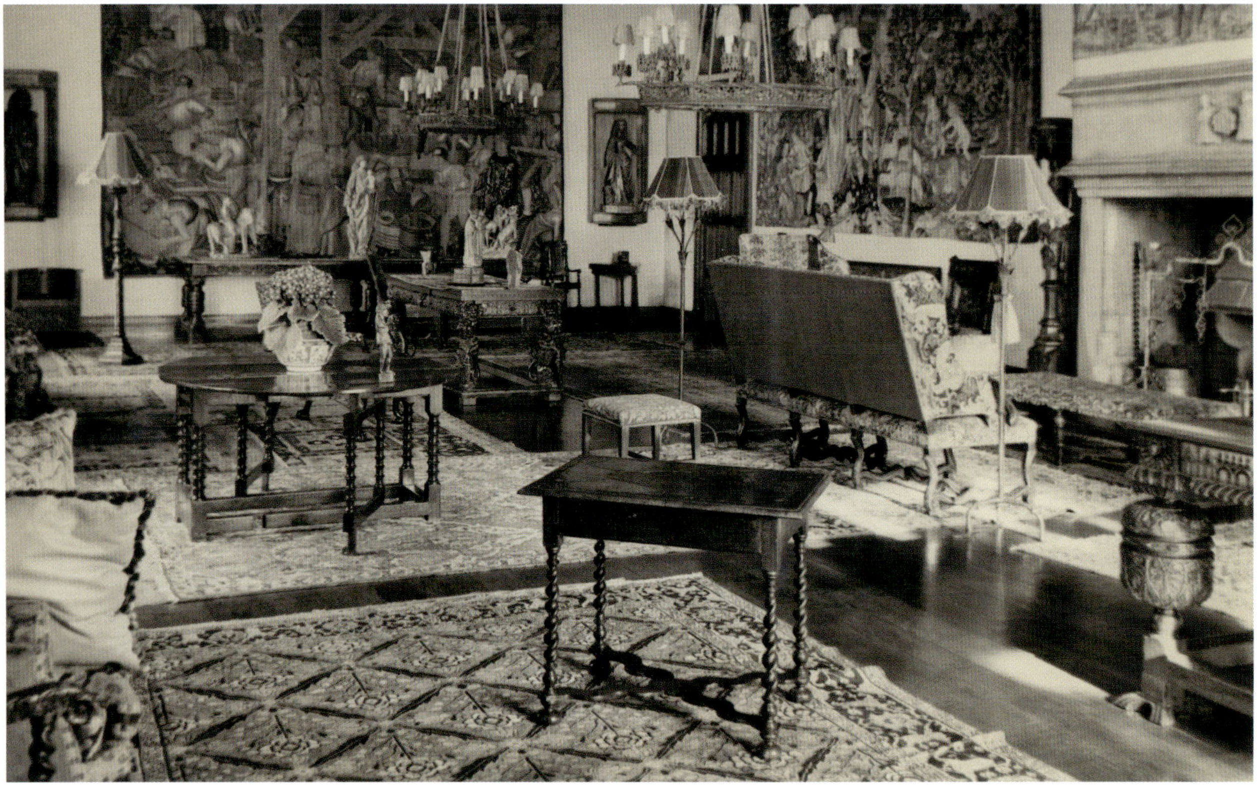

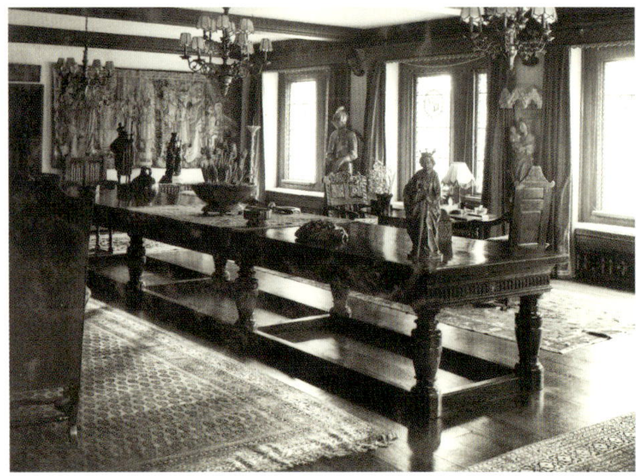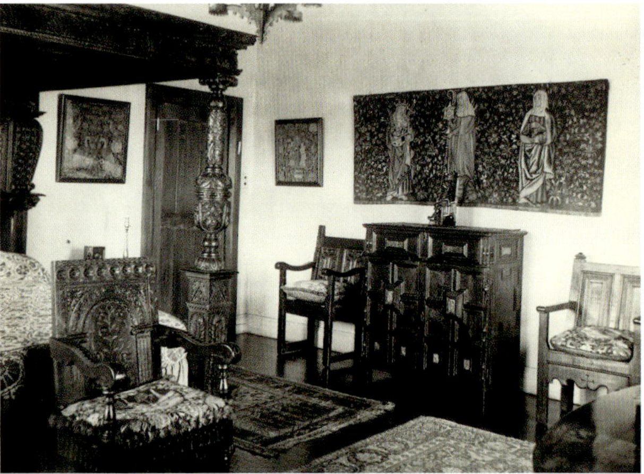

Islamic carpets were used in many rooms in Hutton Castle, William and Constance Burrell's Berwickshire home, as can be seen in these photographs from 1949.

Top: In the drawing room, six large carpets are on the floor and two small ones are on each of the long tables.

Above, left: In the hall, four large carpets surround the large table and a small carpet is on the table.

Above, right: In bedroom no. 2, there are a number of carpets – in the foreground the corner of a large Mughal Indian carpet can be seen, and next to it is an Ottoman Turkish prayer rug.

Photographs by Rupert Roddam. Glasgow Museums Archive, GMA.2013.1.1.1932, GMA.2013.1.1.1939, GMA.2013.1.1.2489.

Introduction

Recalling Sir William Burrell and his collection of Islamic carpets, the distinguished art historian, museum director and broadcaster Lord Kenneth Clark (1903–83) once recounted a conversation between himself and Sir William:

'In the bedrooms at Hutton Castle, I would say, "That's a beautiful carpet, Sir William." "Aye," Burrell would say, "but there's a better one underneath; you'll find a better one underneath." And I tell you, there was a better one. "That's even better!" "Yes," again Burrell would add, "but turn it up; yes, but turn it up again, you'll find an even better one still underneath there." And so it would go on, until about five carpets have been turned up, you see!'

Over a lifetime of collecting Burrell purchased more than 130 carpets and carpet fragments that originated in the Islamic cultures of the Middle East, the Caucasus, northern India, Central Asia and beyond, all handmade knotted-pile carpets, including a wide variety of types and dating from the sixteenth to the nineteenth centuries. These luxury floor coverings were not only used to furnish his homes, but also included many examples of rare and early carpets that he recognized as being important, worthy of being collected despite some being worn or only a section of a larger original carpet. Burrell's pile carpets form part of a larger group of Islamic material he collected, which includes ceramics, metals, velvets and embroideries, dating from the tenth to the nineteenth centuries.

Burrell's correspondence tells of him lending carpets for display in Glasgow and other cities, from Perth in Scotland to Leicester and Ipswich in England. His earliest recorded loan was to the 1901 Glasgow International Exhibition, where eight of his Islamic carpets were displayed in the Fine Art section.

Later, a loan by Glasgow Museums in September 1954 allowed Glasgow Cathedral to be laid out with seven carpets and draped with four tapestries from the Burrell Collection, on the occasion of a royal visit from Queen Elizabeth The Queen Mother (1900–2002). It was reported in the newspapers that she was delighted with the whole appearance of the cathedral that day; this pleased Sir William and Andrew Hannah (1908–78), the first keeper of the Burrell Collection, who exchanged letters about the visit.

After Sir William and Constance, Lady Burrell had gifted much of their collection to the city of Glasgow in 1944, Sir William remained actively involved in working out how best to display and preserve it. For the carpets, Burrell advised on the types of rollers and dust sheets to be used for their storage, and on how to prevent and deal with moth infestation. From a preservation perspective, Burrell recognized the difference between use of the carpets within his private homes and exhibiting them in a public space. He advocated that all the carpets be displayed hung on walls, arguing that laying them flat could cause them to be 'badly injured' by people accidentally walking over them.

Burrell's keenness for the artistic importance of pile carpets to be recognized and for them to be treated as seriously as tapestries is best illustrated by some of his letters, dating from 1948 and 1949, to the keepers of his collection at Glasgow Museums, in which he persisted in gently urging them to prepare a souvenir booklet about the carpets, to be part of a series published for a major exhibition of objects that the Burrells had gifted to the city, held at the McLellan Galleries, Glasgow, in 1949. Unfortunately, this request was not fulfilled. It is hoped that this book will now realize this wish.

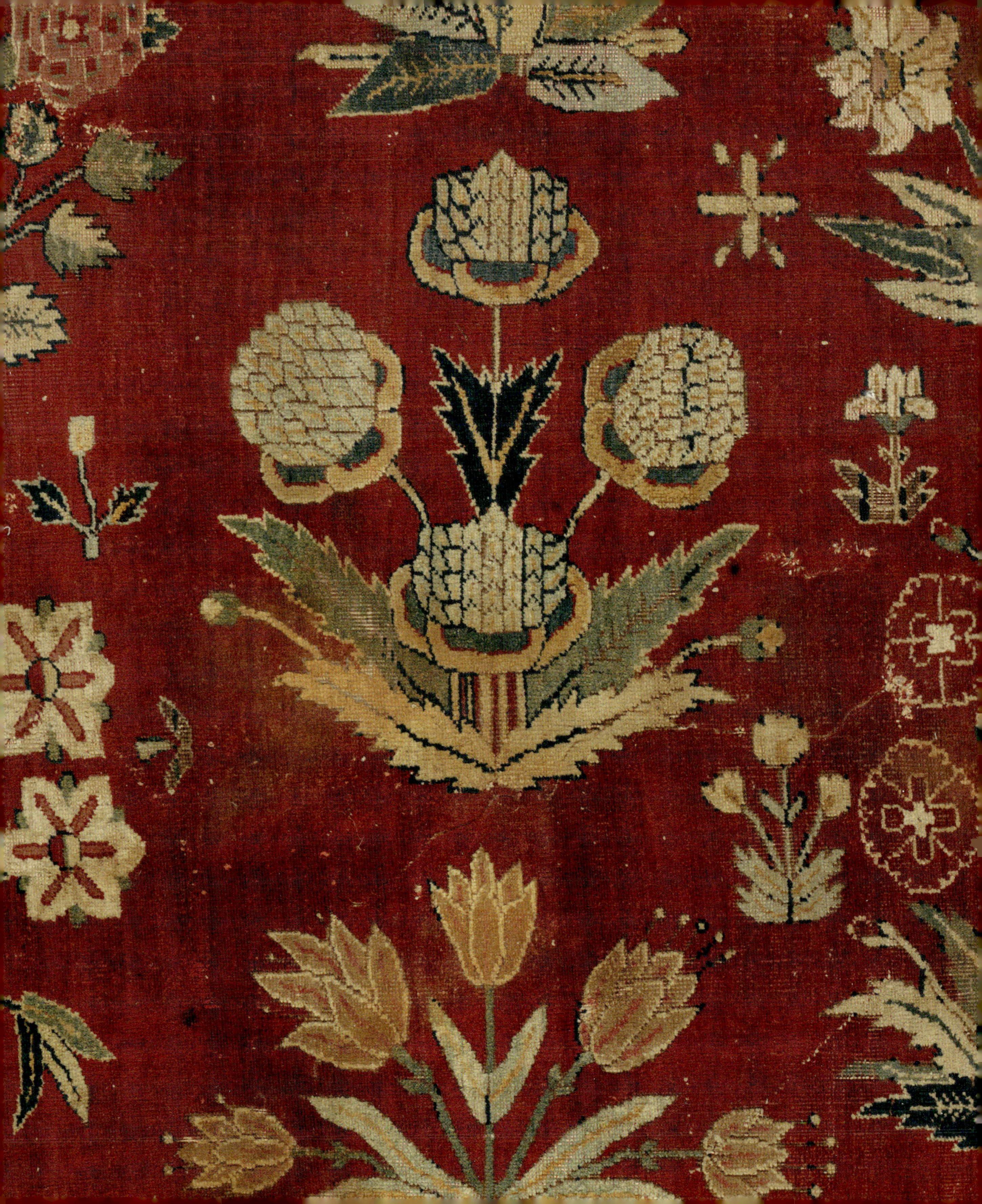

A Garden for Indoors

For the peoples of the Middle East and Central Asia, during the warm months of the year the gardens of both the humble home and the grand palace play an important role in daily life. The garden is not only a place for relaxation and pleasure, but also where many domestic activities take place and where a variety of fruits are grown. When winter sets in and gardens lose their warmth, vegetation and colour, people move their activities indoors, but conjure up their gardens' atmosphere and qualities through winter-season floor coverings – pile carpets with a soft and warm feel, which provide a pleasurable surface to walk and sit on. These knotted-pile carpets are filled with colourful floral and vegetal designs that brighten the bleak season and evoke the beauty of nature in full bloom.

Knotted-pile carpets are handmade textiles created according to local traditions of manufacture, which depend on inherited techniques of making and the materials and colour dyes available. Their construction involves stretching warp threads, usually of cotton or wool, over vertical or horizontal looms. Around each pair of warps are hand tied little lengths of thread – of wool or silk – that make tufts of pile, which are commonly known as knots. After each row of knots has been completed, shoots of thread, the wefts, are passed between the warps – alternately in front of and behind, or over and under, each warp thread – and beaten down against the pile knots to compress the rows as tightly as possible. These weft threads may be singular or multiple shoots of wool, cotton or silk, or any combination of the three. Then a further row of knots is added to the warps, followed by weft threads, and the process is repeated until the carpet reaches its desired size.

In today's visual language, each knot of pile is akin to a square on graph paper or a pixel on a computer screen. The finer and more closely positioned the threads used in the warp and weft and pile, the more knots can be crammed into a square inch or centimetre, and the more finely detailed the motifs can be in the design chosen for the carpet.

Carpet designs follow traditional conventions. These determine the general layout of the carpet – which is commonly divided into a main field and a border made up of a number of frames – and the combinations of motifs and colours which are employed to decorate the various parts. The designs may be implemented from memory, or weavers may follow coloured templates, or instructions may be written down and verbally recited to weavers as they work. The motifs have a variety of origins, from observations of nature, to borrowing from other arts and crafts – including miniature painting, architecture and other types of textiles.

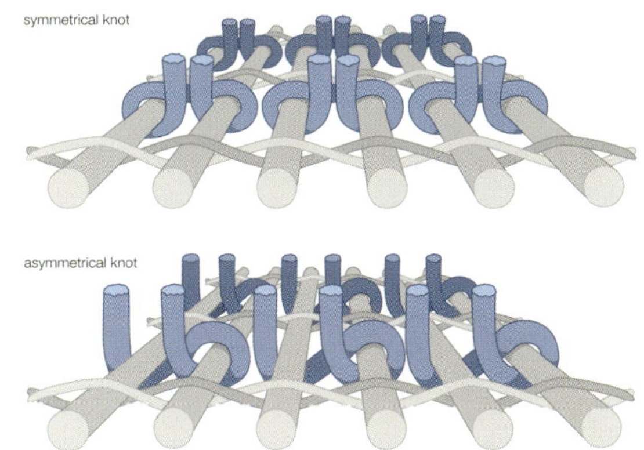

Above: This diagram shows the two main types of knots used for knotted-pile carpets – symmetrical and asymmetrical. The basic structure of all knotted-pile carpets is the same: the warps are the thickest yarns, stretched across the carpet's length; the knots are short yarns tied around pairs of warps; the wefts are thinner yarns woven between the warps, alternating with rows of knots. Illustration from *Encyclopaedia Britannica* (detail).

Opposite: These realistically illustrated flowers are from a Mughal Indian carpet, inspired, like many Islamic carpets, by the beauty of nature found in gardens. Detail from carpet 9.12 (p. 48).

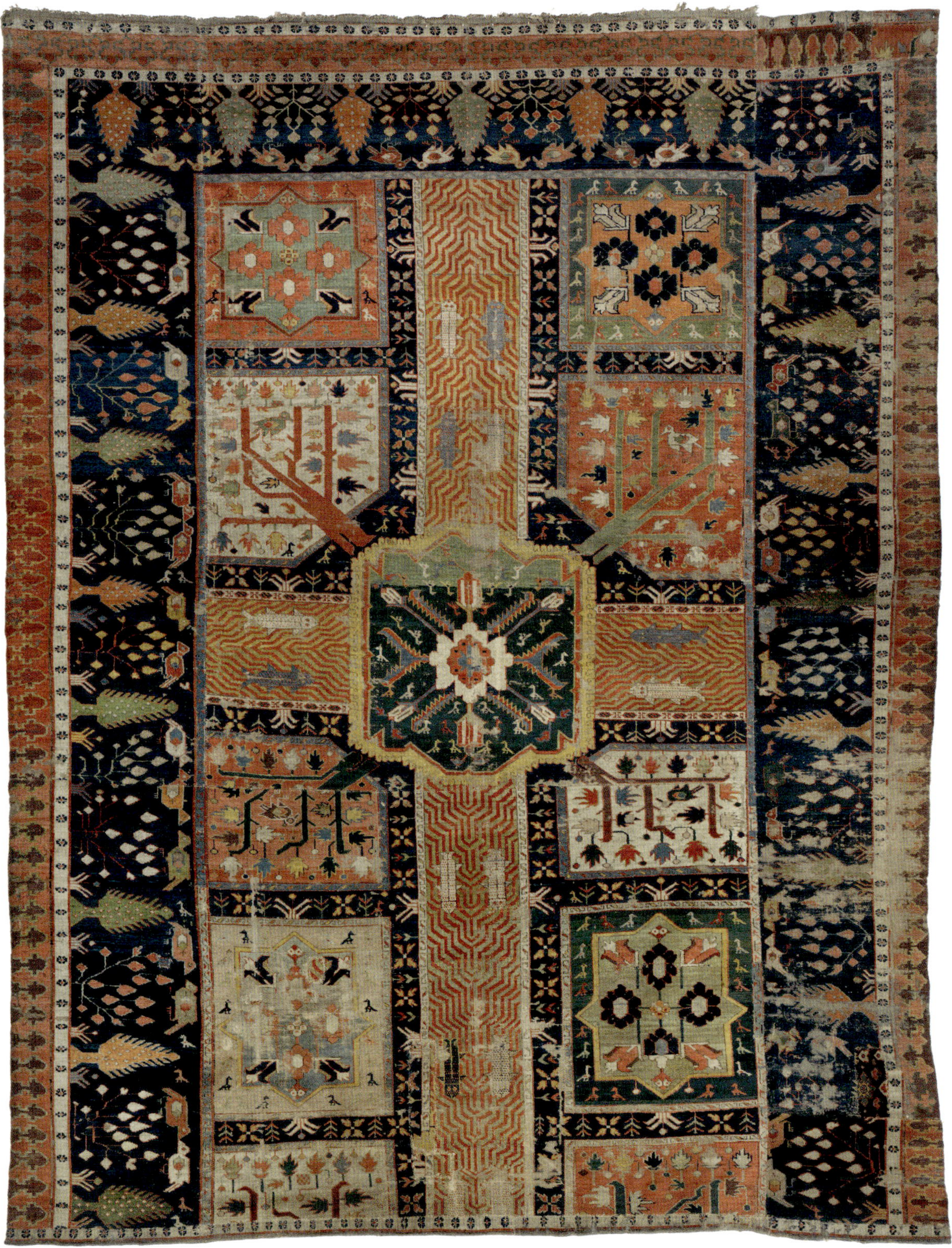

Chahar-Bagh carpet fragment,

Safavid period, about 1600–1700
Made in north-west Iran
Cotton warps and wefts; wool pile
431.8 x 337.8 cm
9.9

A third of the size of the original carpet, this carpet fragment features the theme of the *Chahar-Bagh* – the term in the Persian language for the four-quartered walled gardens of ancient Iran – which on the complete carpet would have been repeated multiple times. The *Chahar-Bagh* design is inspired by both the layout of Iran's ancient gardens and by the description in the Qur'an of Paradise, with its four waterways, itself of biblical origin. On this carpet fragment, four wide water channels, shown in red and yellow, divide the garden into four sections, each containing smaller square gardens with trees and floral compositions. Zigzag lines represent the ripples of water in the channels, where pairs of fish, blue and white, swim. Where the waterways meet, an island garden is placed. This *Chahar-Bagh* is surrounded by a band of cypress trees, amongst which there are birds and shrubs.

In his correspondence, Burrell wrote about his appreciation of this carpet, and he displayed it in several places, including at the 1901 Glasgow International Exhibition.

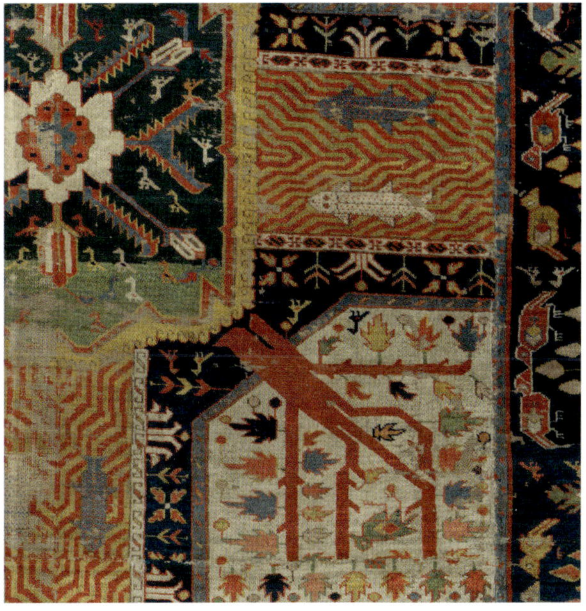

On the green island where the waterways meet, little white birds can be seen standing amongst the flowers. On the dark-blue background of the border, larger red and yellow birds perch on the tops of trees and bushes.

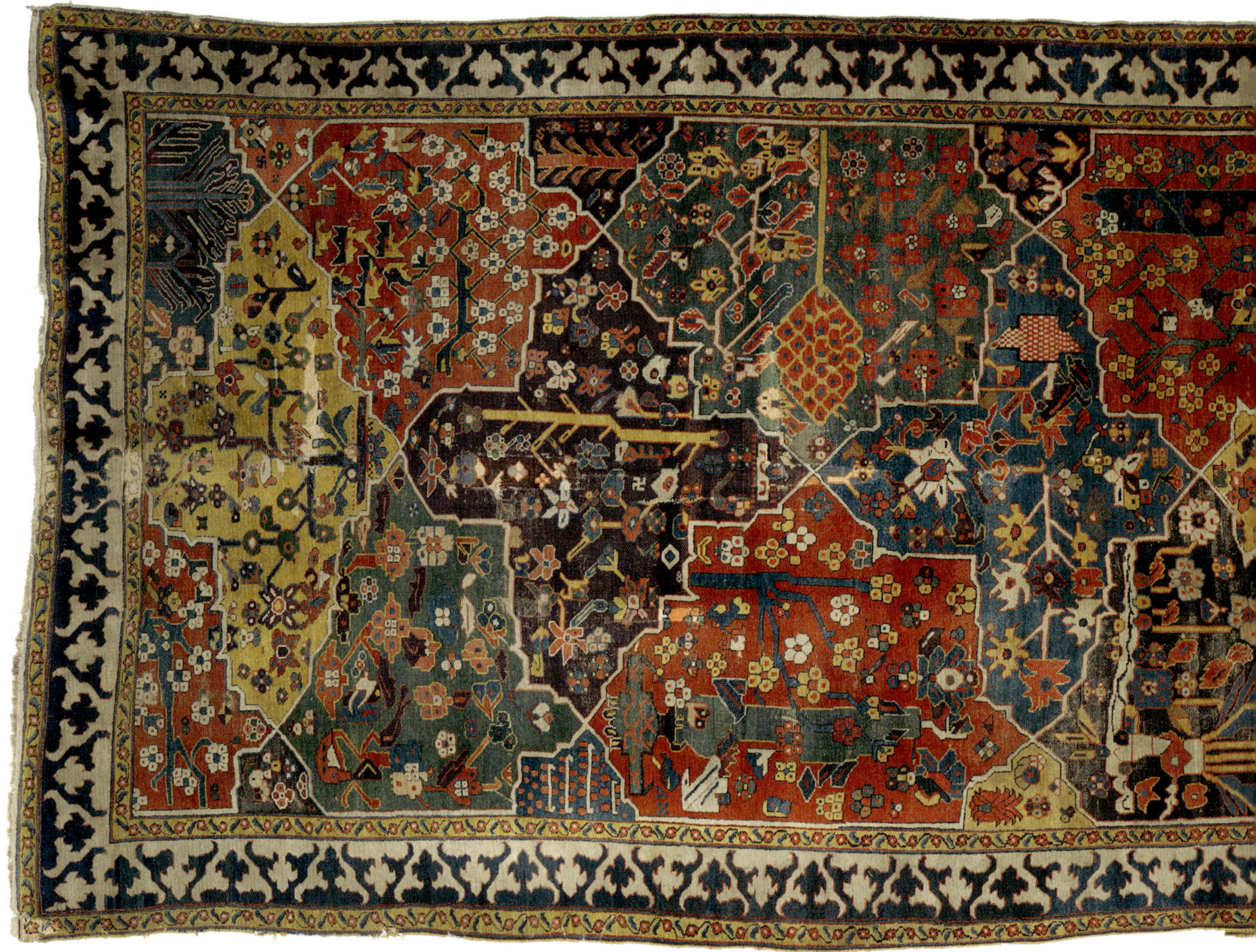

Tree and shrub cartouche carpet,
about 1700–1800
Made in north-west Iran
Wool warps and wefts; wool pile
612.1 x 210.8 cm
9.90

Fifteen small gardens occupy the field of this carpet, one in each of its multicoloured cartouches, or compartments. In each garden there is a small stream with a tree growing on its bank surrounded by shrubs and flowers. These miniature gardens are not orientated in the same direction, with some in an upside-down position in relation to adjacent gardens, so that the carpet can be enjoyed from every direction. The garden compartments here are based on an original design of interlocking crosses and eight-pointed stars, but the weaver, when loosely following the design, has enlarged the cross-shaped compartments – presumably to better show the gardens in them – and caused the shapes of all the cartouches to appear distorted.

Burrell bought this carpet in 1916 from the Armenian dealer Mirhan Krikor Gudenian (1870–1921), one of a number of carpet dealers of Ottoman origin based in London.

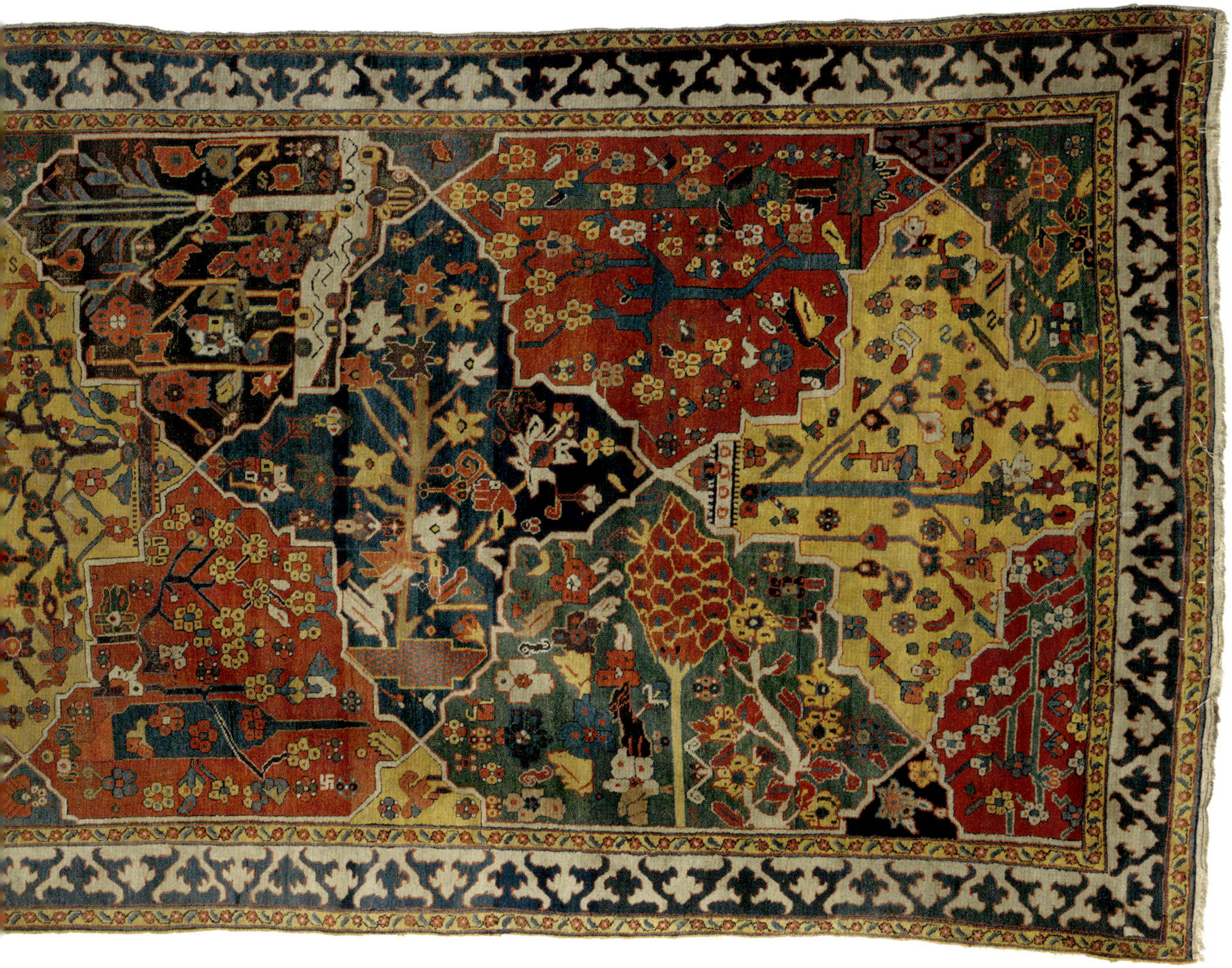

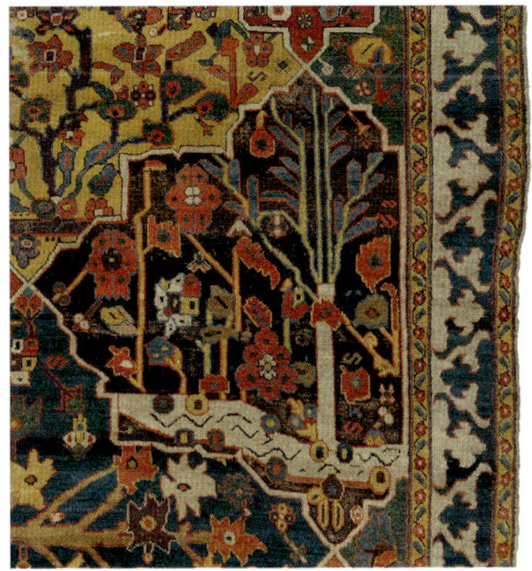

Right: In one of the gardens occupying a star-shaped cartouche on this carpet stands a tree on the bank of a stream, surrounded by flowering shrubs and set against a very dark-blue, almost black, background.

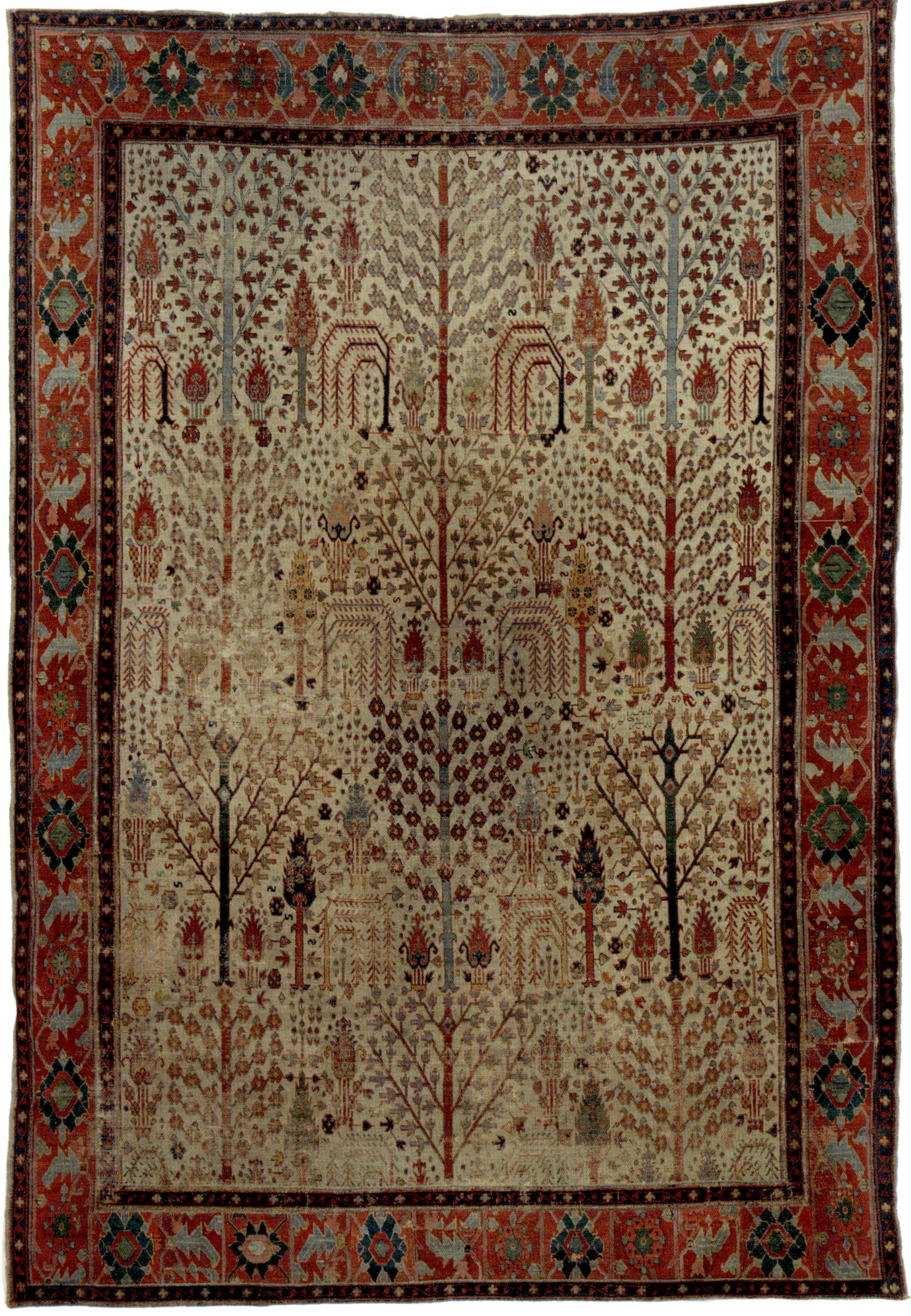

Shahr Khanum's carpet,

about 1700–1800
Made by Shahr Khanum in western Iran
Cotton warps and wefts; wool pile
459.7 x 325.1 cm
9.75

A well-ordered orchard garden of blossoming fruit trees, weeping willows and cypresses is the subject of this carpet. The willow trees, with their distinctive fronds, give this design its name in the Persian language – *Bid Majnun* (Weeping Willow). Hidden amongst the trees, halfway up the right side, just between the top of the dark-blue tree and below the red-trunked tree, is a three-word inscription that the carpet weaver chose to humbly weave into her carpet, which translates to: 'made by Shahr Khanum'. This inclusion of a maker's name is a very rare occurrence, especially surprising when added by a female weaver.

At some point – before Burrell purchased this carpet in 1926 from the carpet dealers Roffe & Raphael of Vigo Art Galleries in London – the length of the carpet was reduced, probably because of damage to the bottom of the field, and the lower border was rearranged.

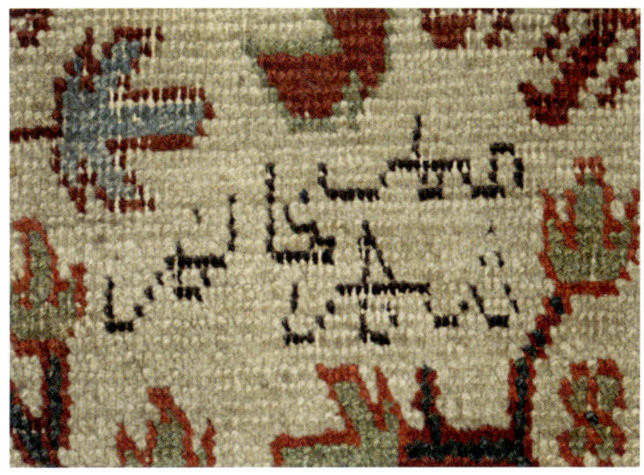

Above and below: Three words in Persian script are woven in black thread on the ivory-coloured background of this carpet, above one of the dark-blue trees. They say '*amal Shahr Khanum*' ('made by Shahr Khanum').

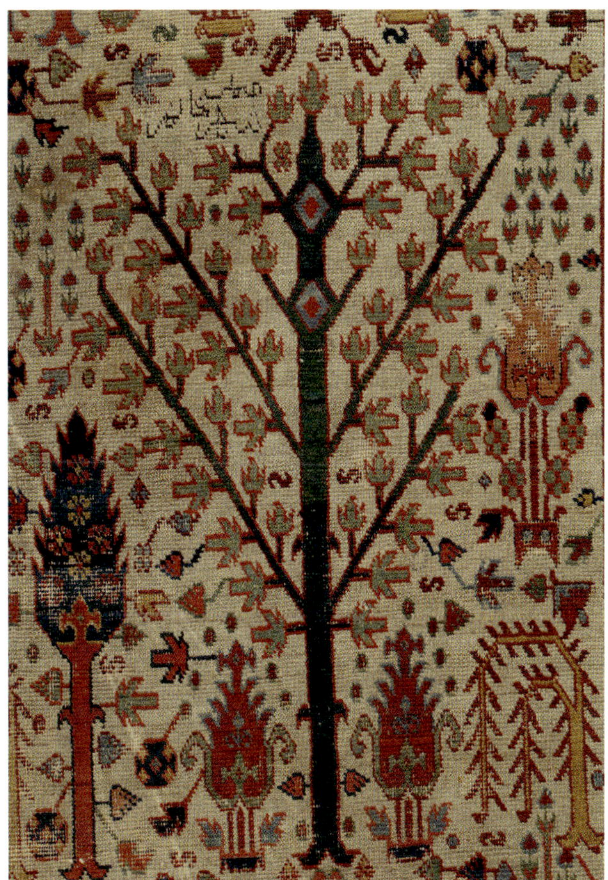

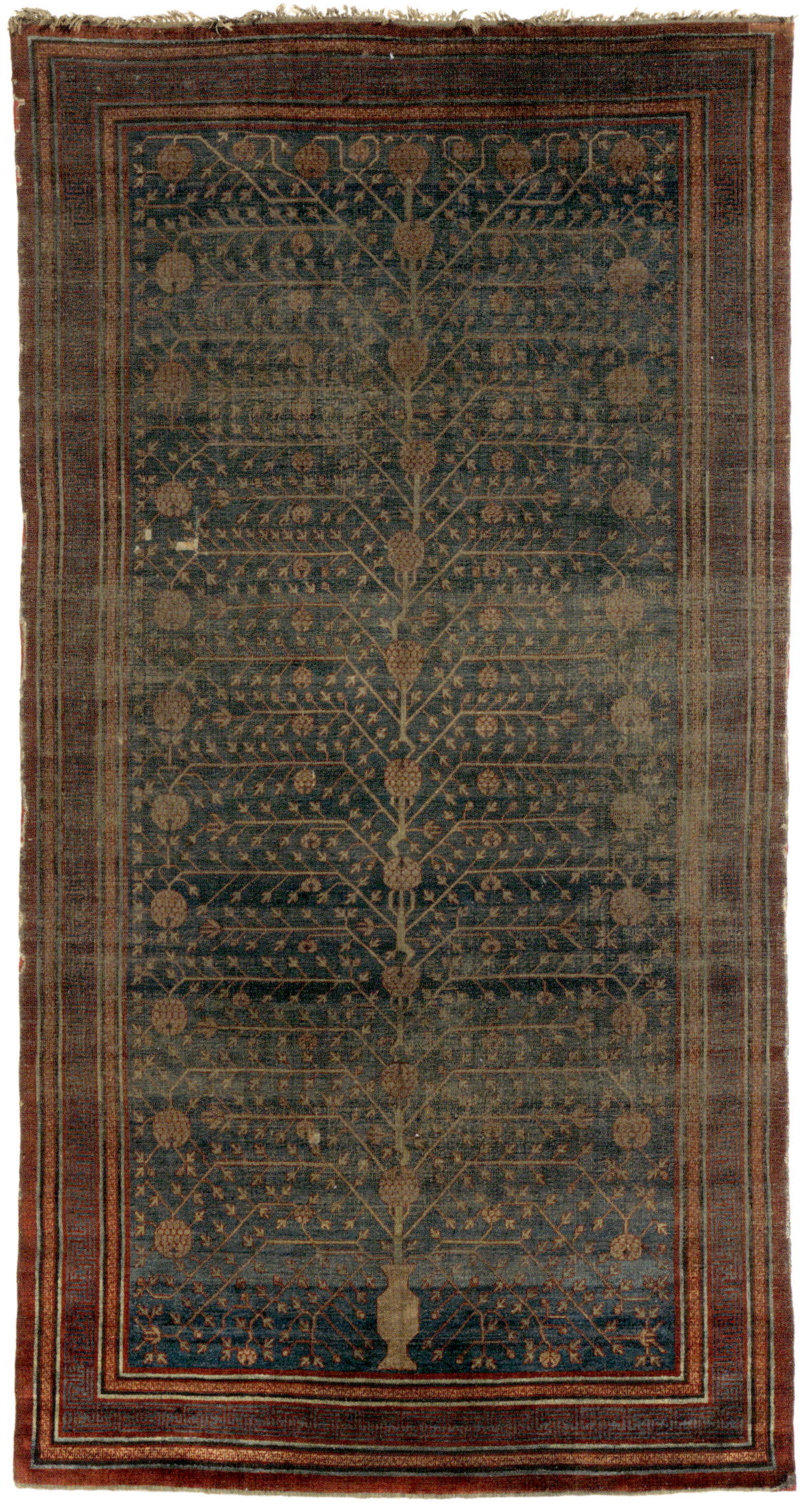

Pomegranate tree carpet,

Qing period, about 1800
Made in Khotan in the historic region of East Turkistan
(today in the Xinjiang Uyghur Autonomous Region, China)
Cotton warps and wefts; silk pile
335.3 x 172.8 cm
9.85

Fruit trees are a must in every garden in the Middle
East and Central Asia, regardless of their size or
location. Here, a delicate pomegranate tree grows
out of a small vase at the base of this silk-pile
carpet. Its leafy, fruit-bearing branches stretch
out upwards and horizontally from the tree's main
stem, filling the whole field.

The pomegranate tree is an ancient symbol of
fertility and abundance. In this depiction, the
insides of the fruits are shown, with their densely
packed faceted seeds. In Islamic culture, God
and his creation are compared to a pomegranate
and its seeds – it being one and holding multitudes.
The swastika-like motif in the main band of the
carpet's border comes from the exposure of Khotan
Muslim carpet weavers to East Asian Buddhist
art, in which this symbol stands for the heart of
Buddha and eternity.

The delicate silk pile of this carpet has suffered
the wear of two centuries of use, giving the false
impression that its colours have faded. In fact, the
colours of its silken pile are still as vibrant as they
were when first dyed, but the pile has become so
worn down that it has exposed the undyed warps
and wefts that lie beneath it, giving the appearance
of faded colour.

1. Each pomegranate fruit on this carpet is shown cut open,
some, as here, with pink seed clusters outlined in red.
2. Individual faceted seeds are depicted within the larger
pomegranates, such as this one.
3. The band of blue swastika-like motifs on a red background
forms the main frame of the carpet's multi-frame border.
4. The pomegranate tree grows from a single vase at the
base of the carpet.

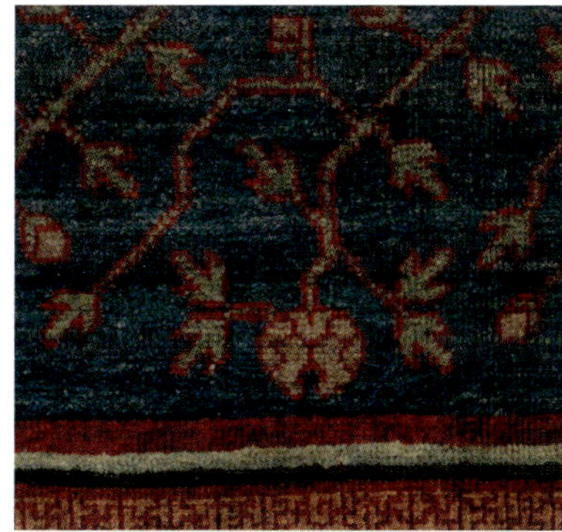

1

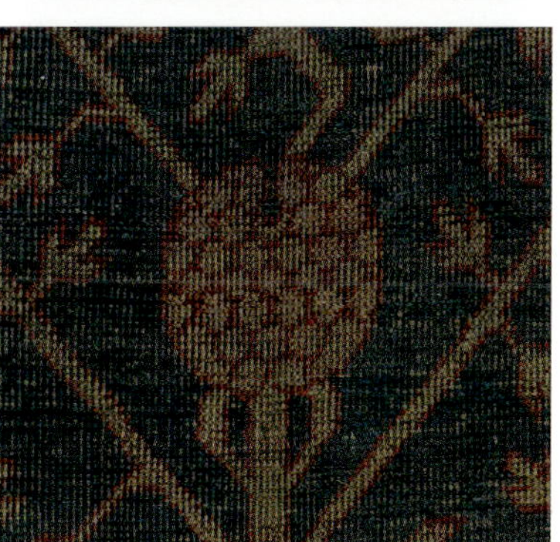

2

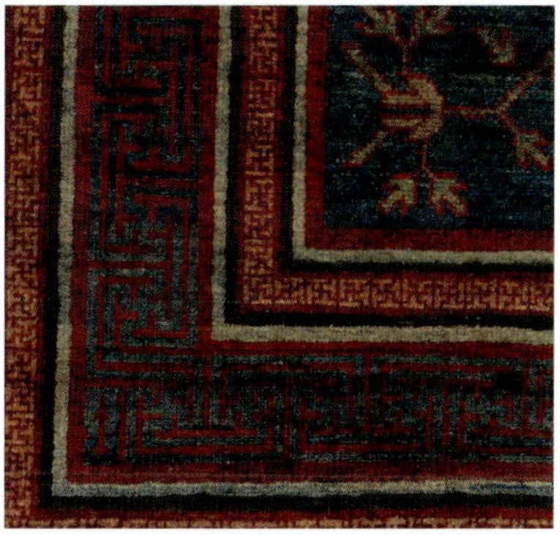

3

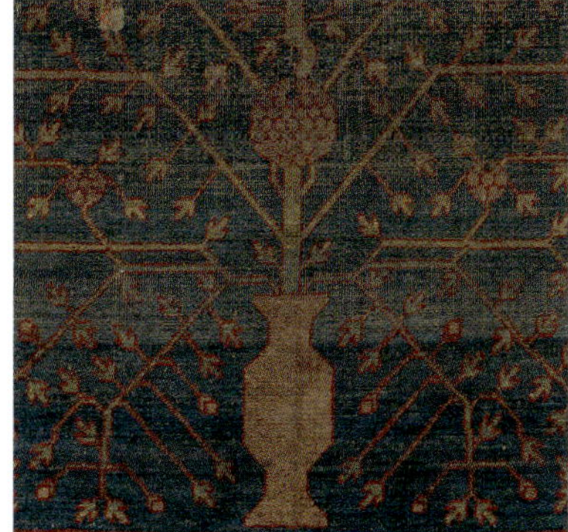

4

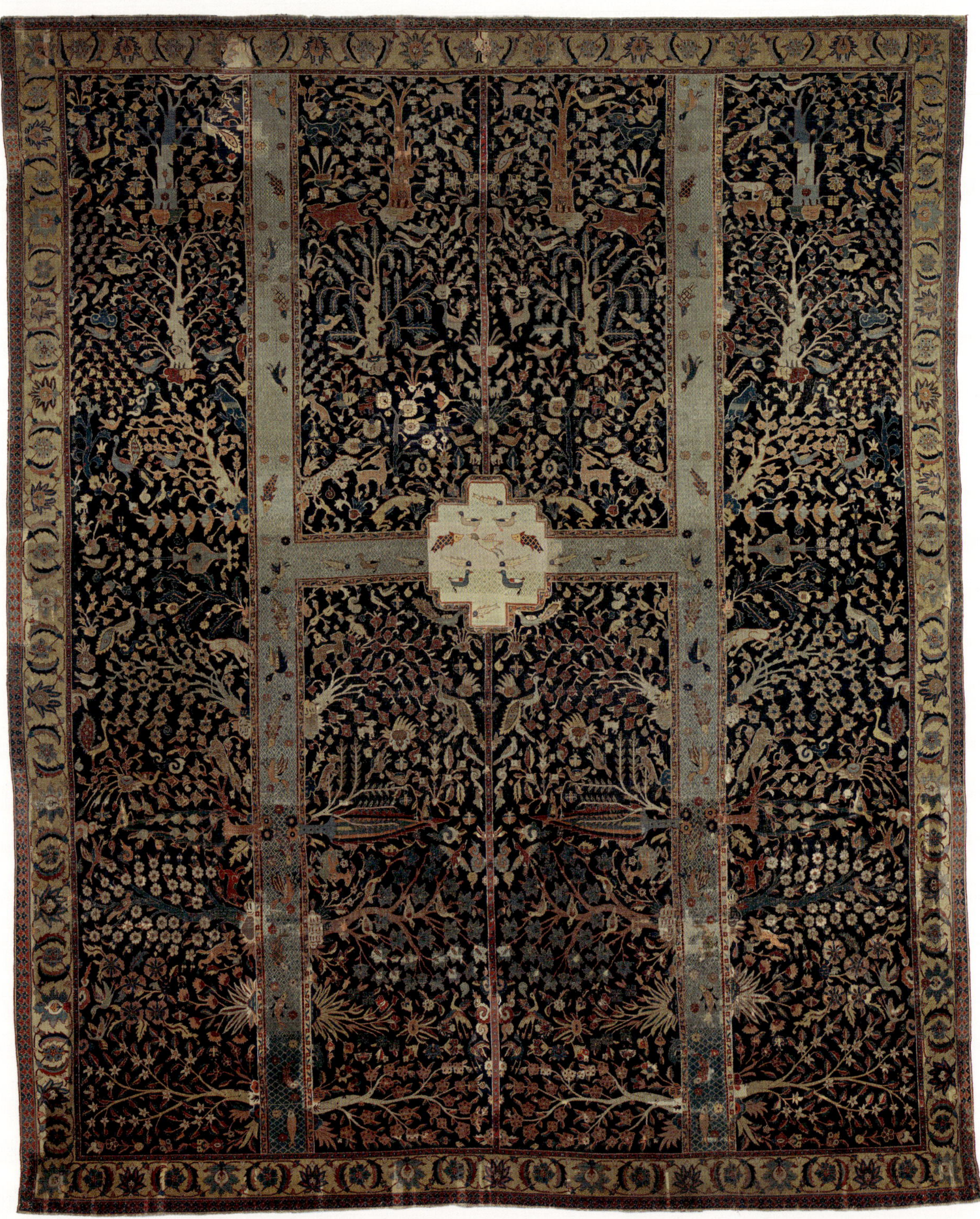

The Wagner garden carpet,

Safavid period, about 1600–1700
Made in Kirman, Iran
Cotton warps, cotton, wool and silk wefts; wool pile
530.9 x 431.8 cm
9.2

Named after its first European owner, the Wagner garden carpet has a layout which recalls the gardens of the ancient Iranians, the Islamic concept of the earthly paradise and the description of heavenly Paradise in the Qur'an. This design shows a walled garden defined by two long parallel water channels linked by two short branch channels and a central pool. Created on a dark-blue background, the garden's six rectangular sections are symmetrical, with the right side of the carpet mirroring its left. On the banks of the waterways on this carpet stand trees, bushes and floral shrubs in full bloom. Animals, birds and multicoloured butterflies and moths inhabit the garden. Fish and ducks populate the waterways, with the shimmering waters ingeniously illustrated by a lattice pattern with varied thicknesses of line and shades of colour.

The unique feature of this carpet design – which perhaps can most easily be appreciated by studying the black-and-white drawing of the carpet to the right – is the gradual change in the orientation of the flora and fauna which occurs from around the middle of the carpet, shifting from being anchored at the edges of the waterways in the lower parts of the carpet to being parallel to them in the upper parts of the carpet. For a person sitting on the bottom half of the carpet, this gradual change of direction would create a panoramic viewing experience. Thus, when the sitter looked around from right to left, they would have the impression of the trees and the animals being in an upright position.

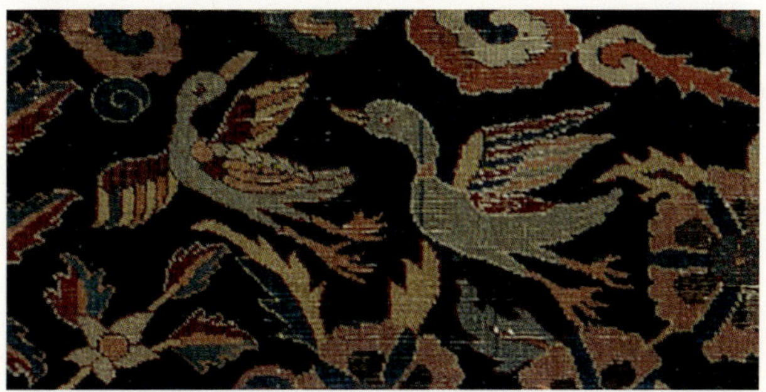

Above: Ducks in flight. They are tucked away near the lower left corner, between the side border, two trees and the top of a large flowering shrub.

Below: This simplified drawing shows the main layout of the carpet. Over the length of the carpet, there is a deliberate gradual change in the orientation of the trees and shrubs, from being at right angles to the water channels near the bottom to parallel to them towards the top. The orientation of the animals and birds also changes.

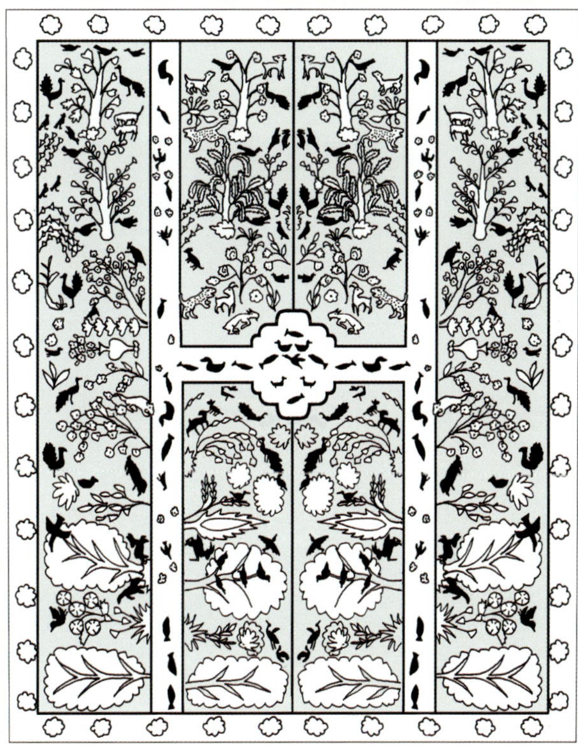

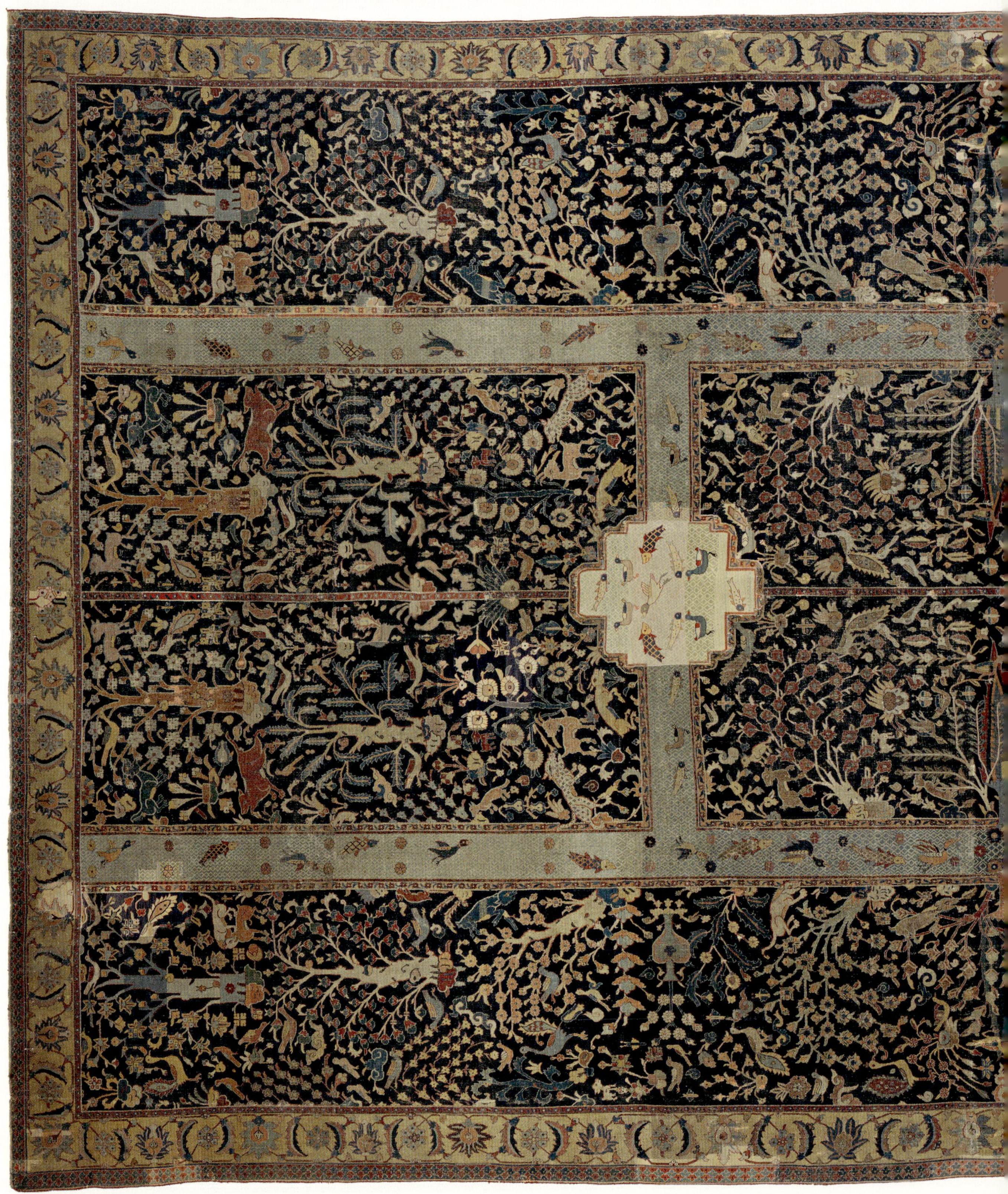

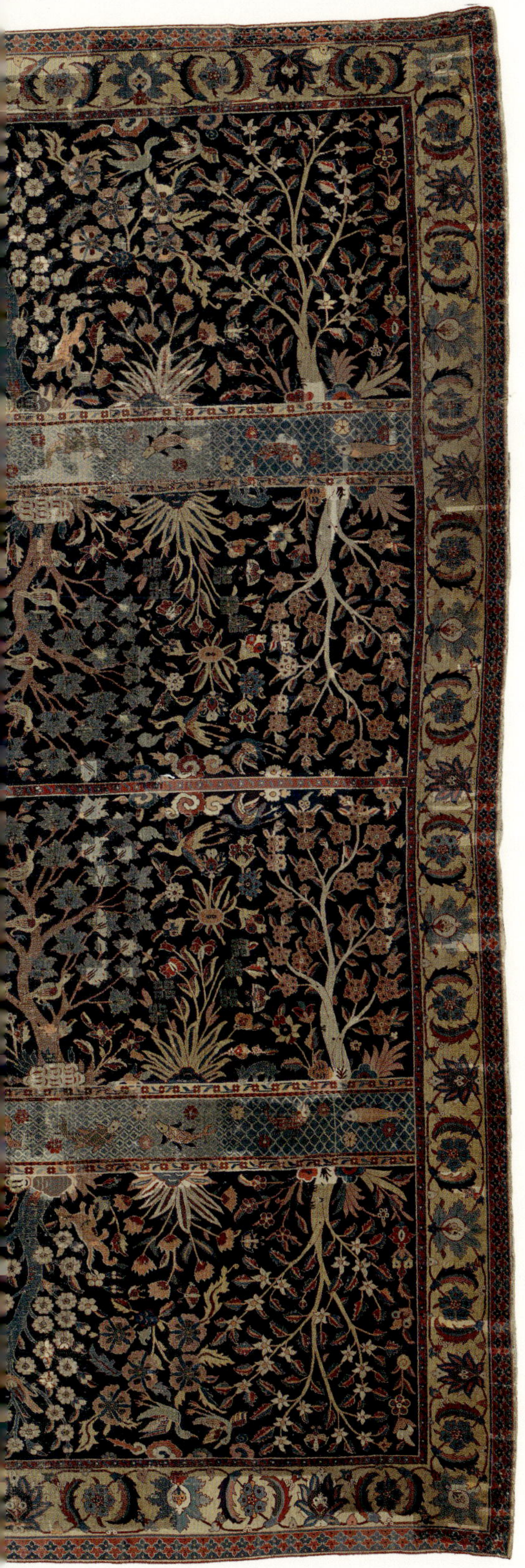

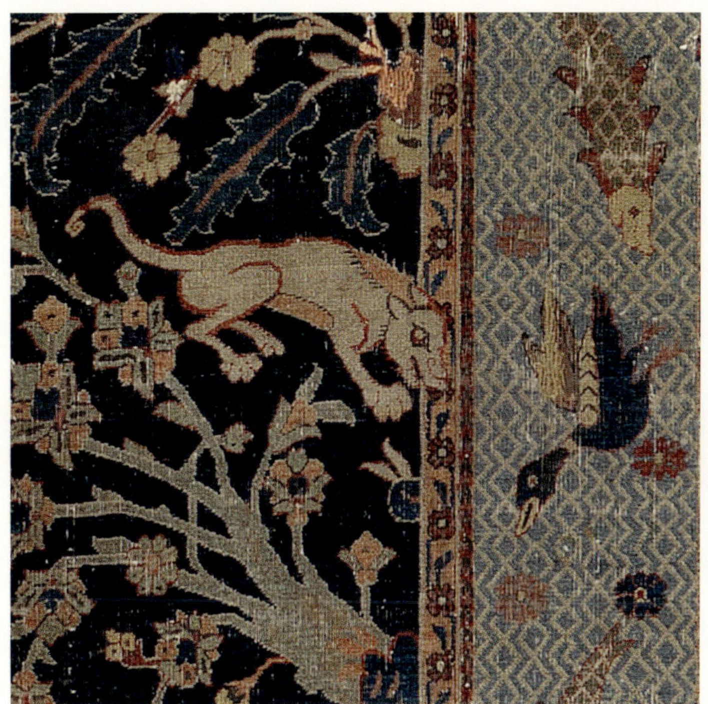

A lion preying on fish and a duck in a stream.

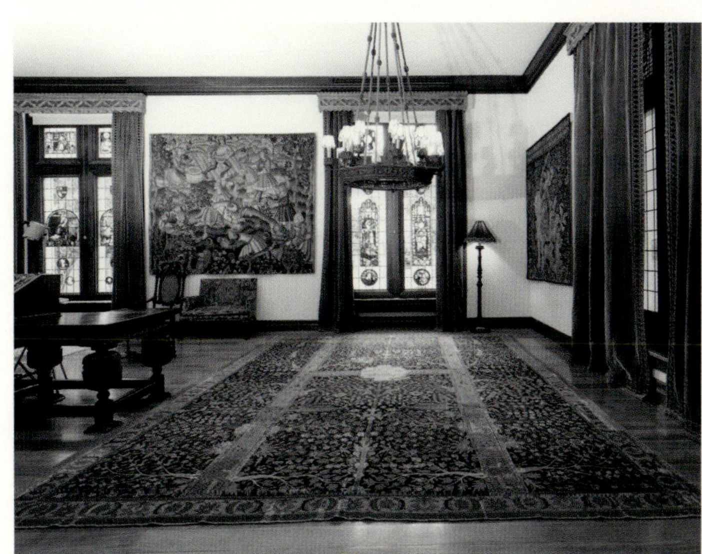

After it was bought by William Burrell, the Wagner garden carpet was placed in a prominent position in the drawing room of Hutton Castle. This photograph from 1990 shows the carpet laid out in a similar position in a reconstruction of the room, which was formerly part of the displays at the Burrell Collection. Glasgow Museums Archive, GMA.2013.1.1.2466.

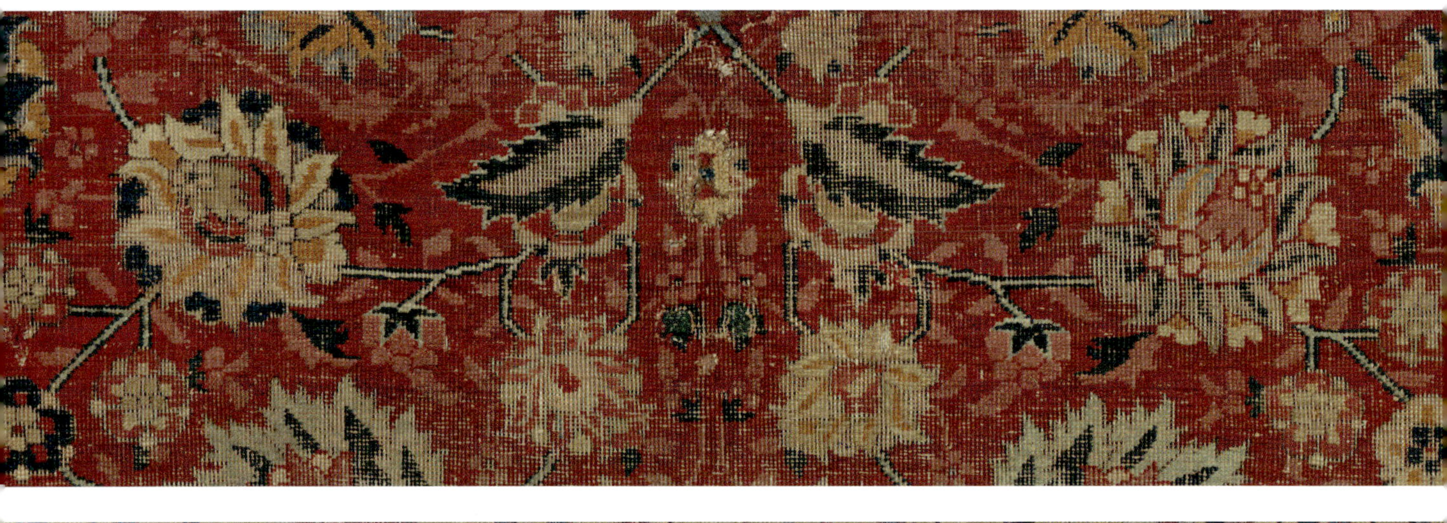

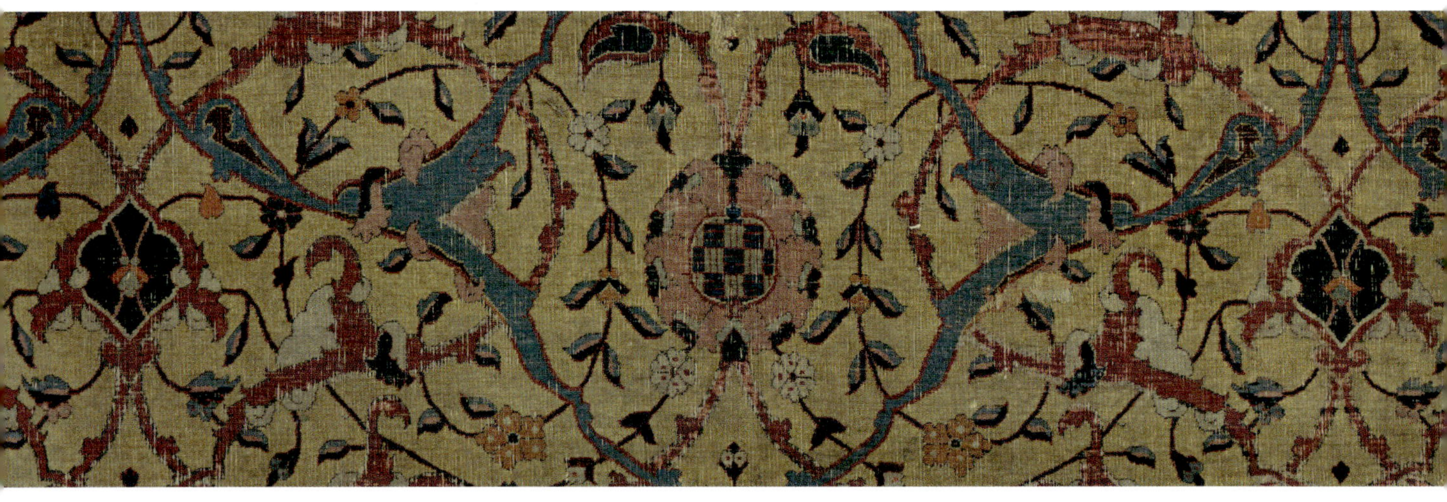

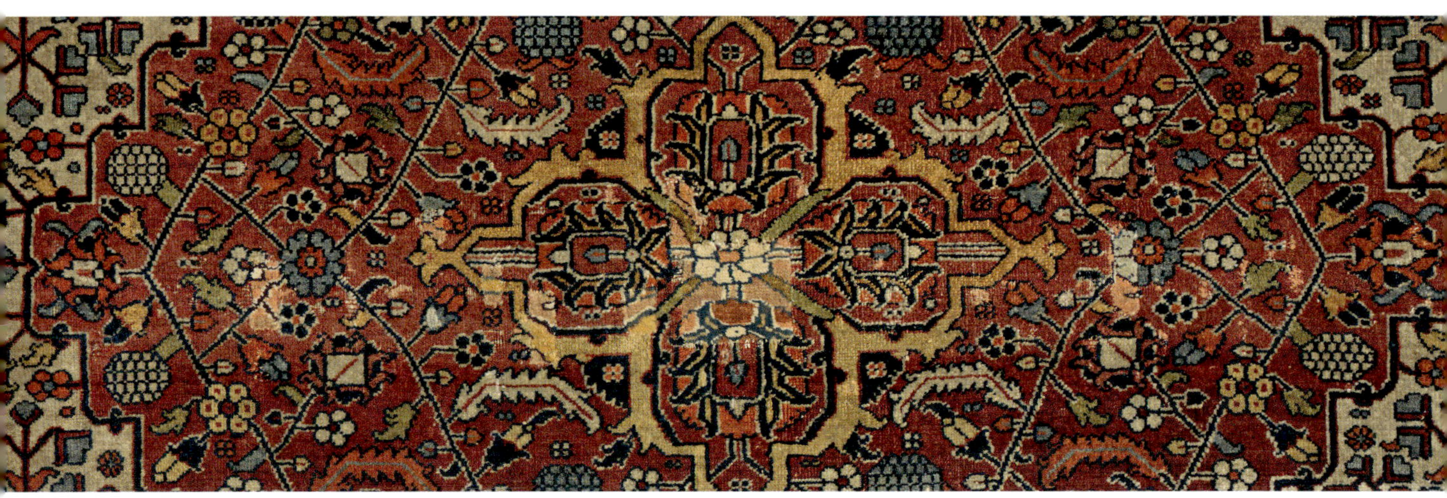

The Arabesque Design

The meandering vine scrolls and the fantastical multicoloured floral motifs known as rosettes and palmettes are the near-ubiquitous decoration of pile carpets from the Islamic world. These vegetal and floral decorative elements are used to create dynamic but balanced lattice patterns that can spread in all directions and, if no border contained them, could infinitely repeat. These richly complex patterns are described as 'arabesque' – a term of French and Italian origin. It was coined to refer to variations of this type of repeated decoration as seen in the arts and crafts of Arab parts of the Islamic world, including the decorative schemes found in the art and architecture of Moorish Spain (the Islamic period in Spain spanned from about 756 to 1609, including the Mudejar era after the end of the Christian reconquest in 1492). Geometric lattice patterns, which appear on buildings and in manuscript decoration and a variety of crafts, and which have a similar ability to repeat seamlessly and endlessly, are also called arabesque but are not commonly used on pile carpets.

While the winding stalks, stems and tendrils of arabesque carpets are reminiscent of the grapevine and similar climbing plants, the imaginative palmettes and rosettes (their names sometimes used interchangeably) are made up of layers of leaves, including palm leaves, and petals in a variety of shapes and colour combinations. These palmettes and rosettes were originally based on stylized Chinese lotus and peony patterns, which were then combined with split-leaf forms to create colourful imaginary flowers. Intertwining and overlapping stalks and stems are used to create individual planes of a lattice. These planes of lattice can be used singly or – like offset layers – multiply, creating complex designs.

An arabesque carpet may also feature a medallion design in the centre of its field. These medallions, with attached pendants, come in various shapes and are usually made up of, or filled in with, arabesque compositions, which add to the richness and complexity of the design. These medallion shapes and the corner pieces and multi-frame borders that come with them were borrowed from the decorative traditions of leather book covers and the illuminated frontispieces of Islamic manuscripts.

The other variation found in early arabesque carpets is the presence of a vase amongst the vegetation and palmettes. Usually one vase, or occasionally several vases, might be found, though in later carpets of this type, none are included. These vases, with shapes influenced by Chinese ceramics, tend to be the source of at least one of the main lattices in the field. Because of their initial presence in early arabesque carpets made in southern Iran and because of the particular weaving technique associated with them – three weft shoots of mixed yarns between each row of knots – the term 'vase carpet' is used to describe this type of carpet from the Safavid period in Iran (1501–1736). Burrell was particularly keen to acquire early carpets from the Safavid period, both whole and fragments, and several important examples grace his collection.

Opposite: Three different approaches to arabesque scroll design are illustrated here: vine scrolls receding into the background, giving prominence to the palmettes they bear (top); vine scrolls given prominence on the field (middle); and a vine-scroll lattice adapted to fit a medallion, diamond-shaped in this example (bottom). Details from carpets 9.33 (p. 31), 9.3 (pp. 24–25) and 9.74 (p. 40).

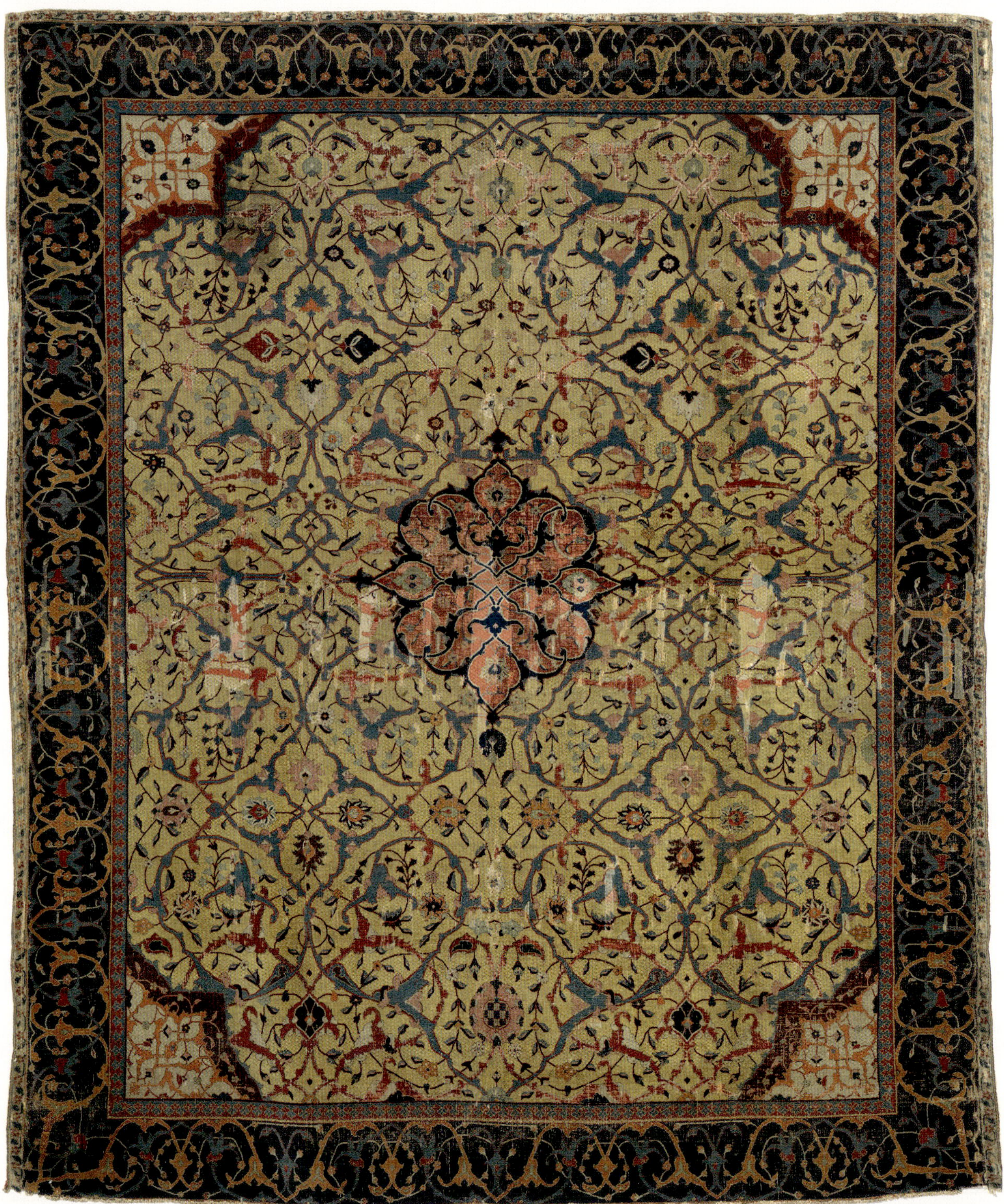

Arabesque carpet with medallion design,

Safavid period, about 1600–1700
Made in Kirman, Iran
Cotton warps, cotton and wool wefts; wool pile
347.9 x 284.5 cm
9.3

A pink medallion sits in the centre of the field of this carpet. From its left and right tips emerges an arabesque network of light-blue vine scrolls bearing pink and maroon leaves. From the top and bottom tips of the medallion emerges a finer arabesque network of dark-blue vine scrolls, which runs under the light-blue vine scrolls and bears multicoloured flowers and palmettes which are positioned in the spaces created by the light-blue scrolls. The pink medallion is also decorated with an arabesque pattern – a thick, dark-blue foliate scroll and a fine, light-blue scroll below it. Quarter medallions are placed in the four corners of the field. They too contain arabesque vine scrolls, one coloured salmon pink and one red, placed on an ivory-coloured background. The subtle presence of these corner pieces with the medallion ensures that they do not overshadow the loveliness of the yellow field with its delicate arabesque lattices. The deep blue of the carpet's border provides a strong contrast and an effective frame to the central field; the three vine scrolls that occupy it intertwine to create a multicoloured chain.

Archival photographs show that Sir William and Constance, Lady Burrell had this carpet laid out in the centre of one of the main bedrooms at Hutton Castle. Glasgow Museums displayed it at least twice during Burrell's lifetime – in 1949 at the McLellan Galleries, Glasgow, and at a second exhibition, also in Glasgow, in 1951.

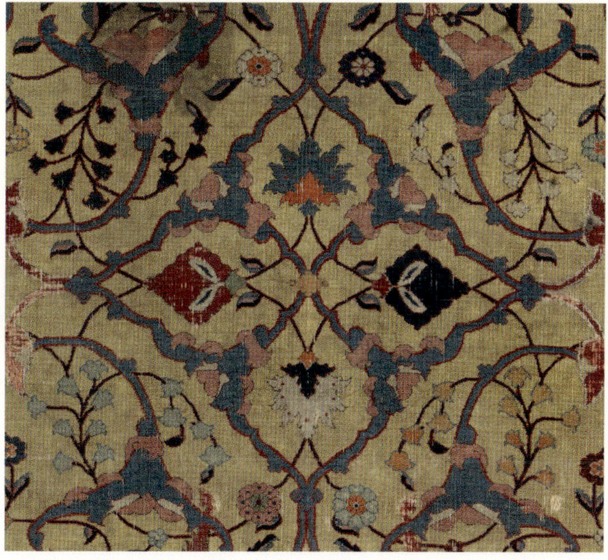

On the field of this carpet, the fine, dark-blue vine scrolls passing under the pale-blue tendrils of the main lattice bear a variety of palmettes, flowers and leaves. Even though these elements are symmetrically distributed, their colours are not, enhancing the dynamism of the arabesque design.

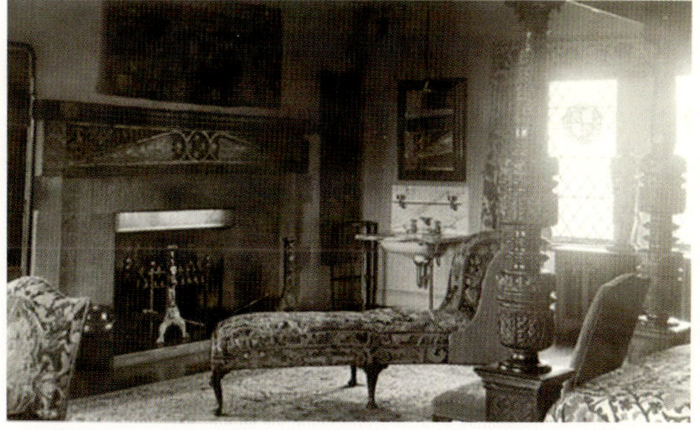

Above: The carpet can be seen laid out in bedroom no. 1 at Hutton Castle in 1949, between the tester bed (the four-poster bed) and the fireplace, with a chaise longue placed on it. Photograph by Rupert Roddam. Glasgow Museums Archive, GMA.2013.1.1.2490.

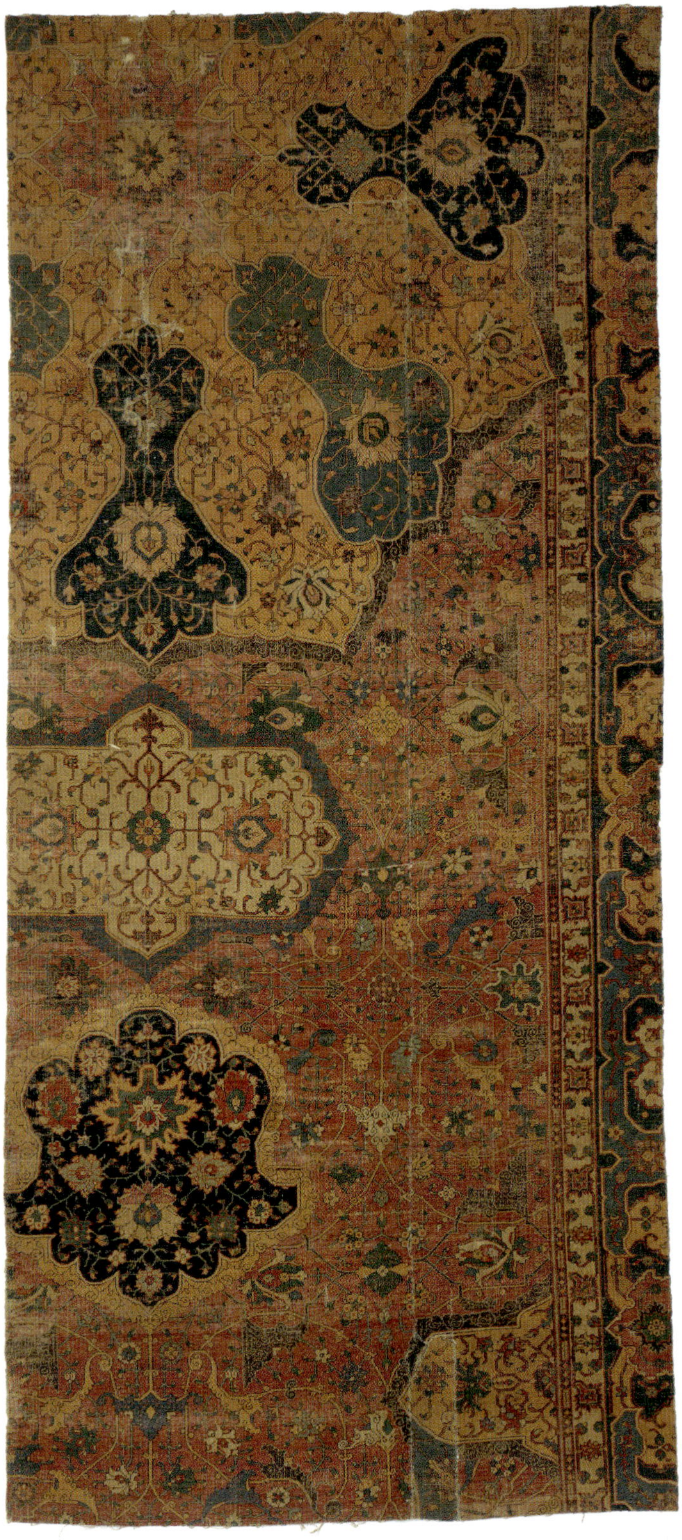

Left: Carpet fragment 9.27: part of the central medallion, field and border of the original carpet.

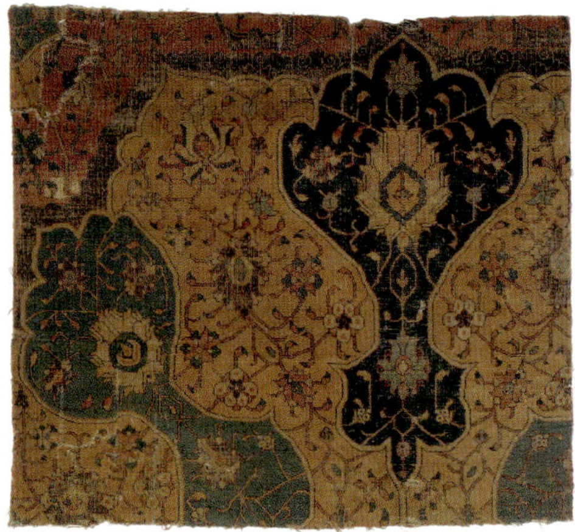

Above: Carpet fragment 9.28: part of the central medallion and field of the original carpet.

Right: In this detail from carpet fragment 9.27, the three-plane lattice – yellow, blue and brown – that covers the red ground of the field can be seen.

Fragments from an arabesque carpet with medallion design,

Safavid period, about 1500–1600
Made in Iran, possibly at Tabriz
Cotton warps and wefts; wool pile
Larger fragment 342.9 x 152.4 cm
Smaller fragment 96.5 x 106.6 cm
9.27, 9.28

These two carpet fragments are from a very large, and, at one time, handsome classic medallion carpet. They show parts of the field and a glimpse of the border. A huge medallion dominates the field and encroaches on the edge of the border. It is made up of interlocking shapes – the dark-blue and turquoise compartments alternating with yellow. Linked to this medallion on its vertical axis are a light-coloured cartouche and a dark-coloured pendant – which would have been mirrored above the medallion on the complete carpet. These devices help visually integrate the medallion into the rectangular field. Every space in the field is filled with multicoloured floral arabesque patterns. In contrast, the border holds two intertwined thick and leafy stem scrolls, one turquoise and the other yellow. The smaller of these two fragments shows part of the central medallion with its interlocking cartouches. Its original position was at the top end of the medallion.

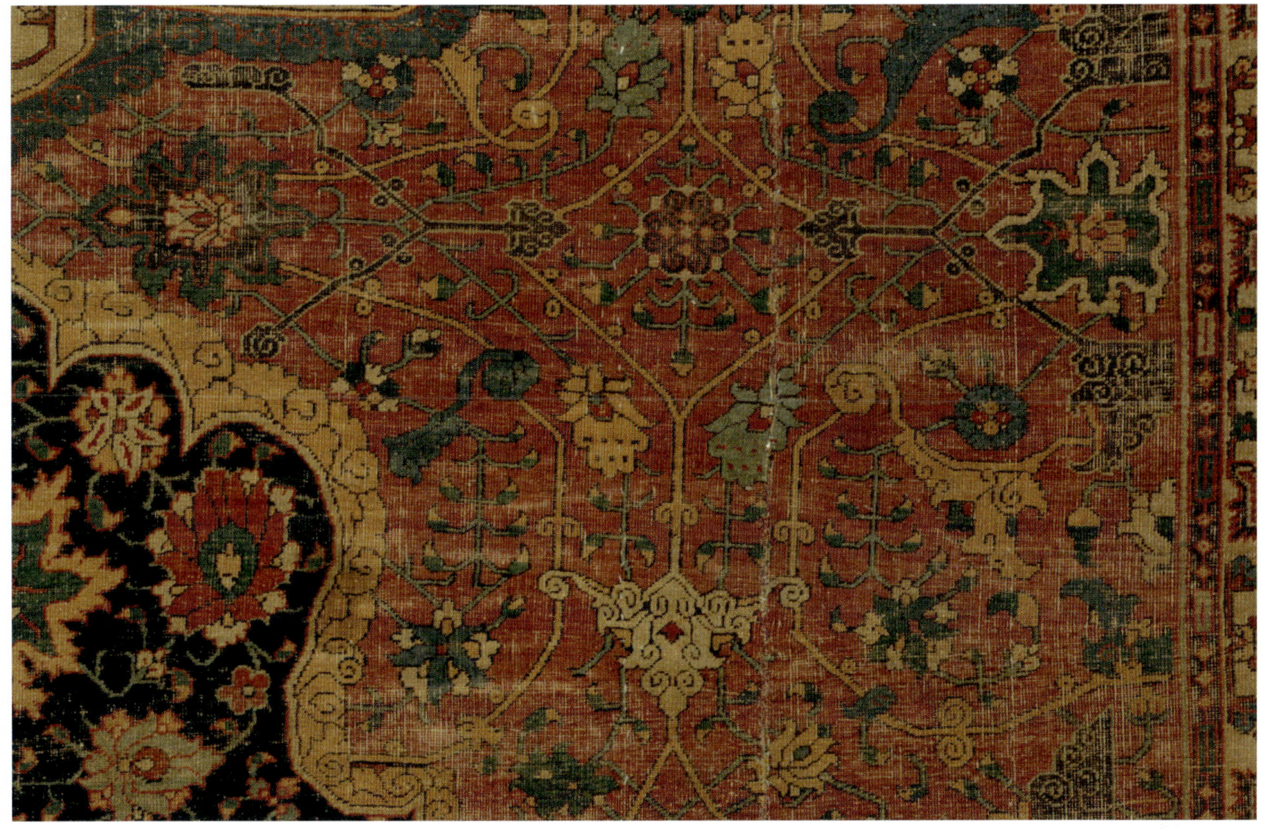

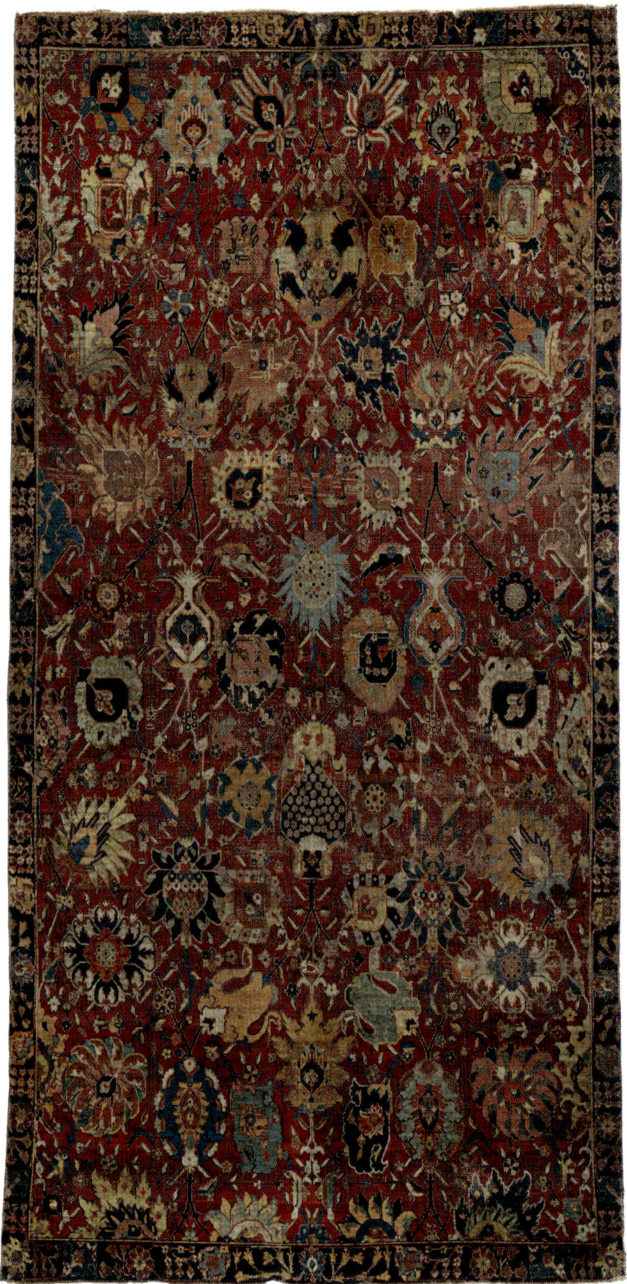

Vase carpet,

Safavid period, about 1600
Made in Kirman, Iran
Cotton warps, wool and cotton wefts; wool pile
358.2 x 175.3 cm
9.6

Just below the centre of this carpet is an upside-down pear-shaped blue vase, decorated with little pink flowers. It acts as the starting point for two of the four overlapping plane lattices that occupy the carpet's field. Even though the design seems crowded and random, a study of the arabesque lattice structure shows a deliberate plan to overlay the red field with the four networks of stems and palmettes. The designer created a symmetrical layout but chose not to distribute the colours in a similar manner. This non-symmetrical use of colour softens the symmetry while preserving the overall balance and charming effect of the carpet.

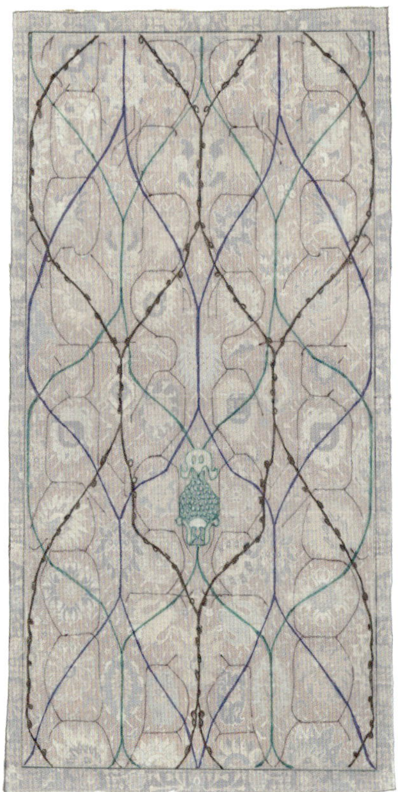

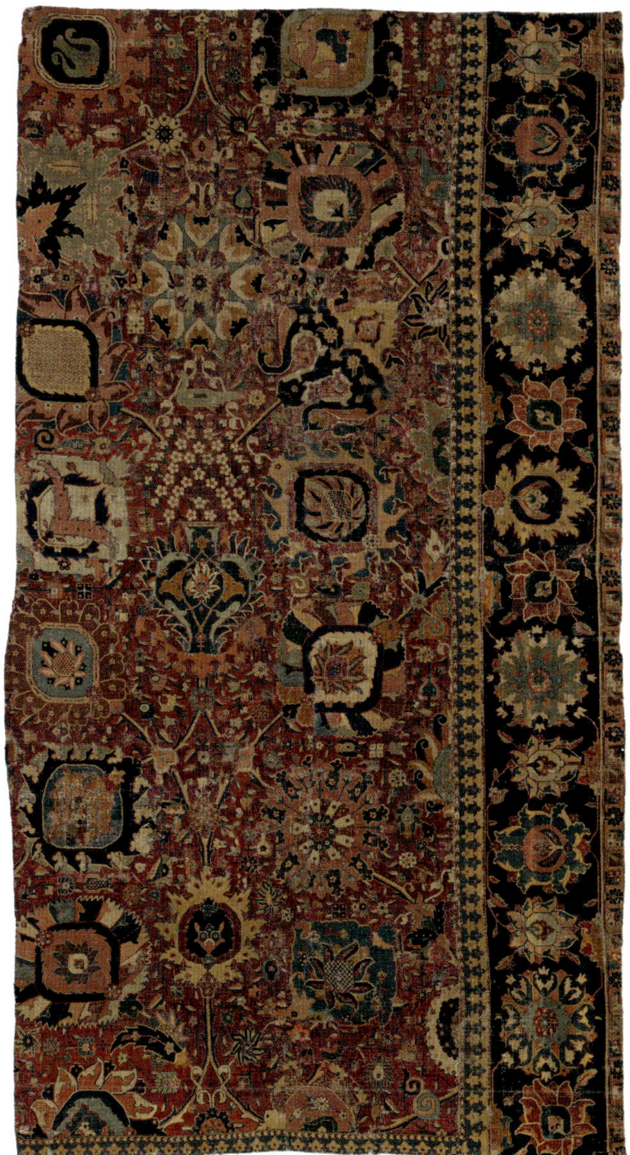

Vase carpet fragment,

Safavid period, about 1600–1700
Made in Kirman, Iran
Cotton warps, wool and cotton wefts; wool pile
320 x 170.2 cm
9.8

Although this fragment of a corner of a carpet's field is from a symmetrically designed carpet, within it no two palmettes look alike. This approach is a deliberate tactic by the designer to create greater movement and maximize the variety of motifs.

Amongst the oversized palmettes there is a blue vase holding a branch of white blossoms. From the top and bottom of the vase emerges the main lattice, its bold stems striped dark blue, pink and cream. Intertwined with it is a second lattice of white, curly tendrils, and, below these two lattices, a fine, blue stem scroll snakes across the red field carrying small flowers, buds and leaves. The designer has also managed to perch a pale-blue pigeon above the white blossoms.

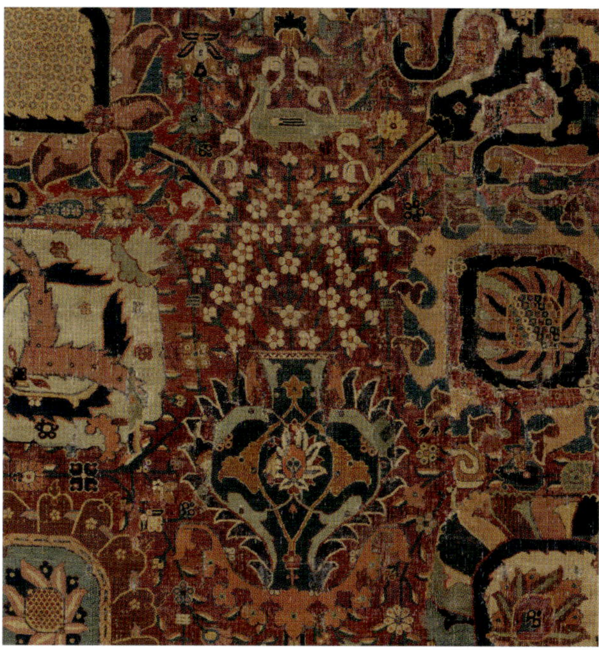

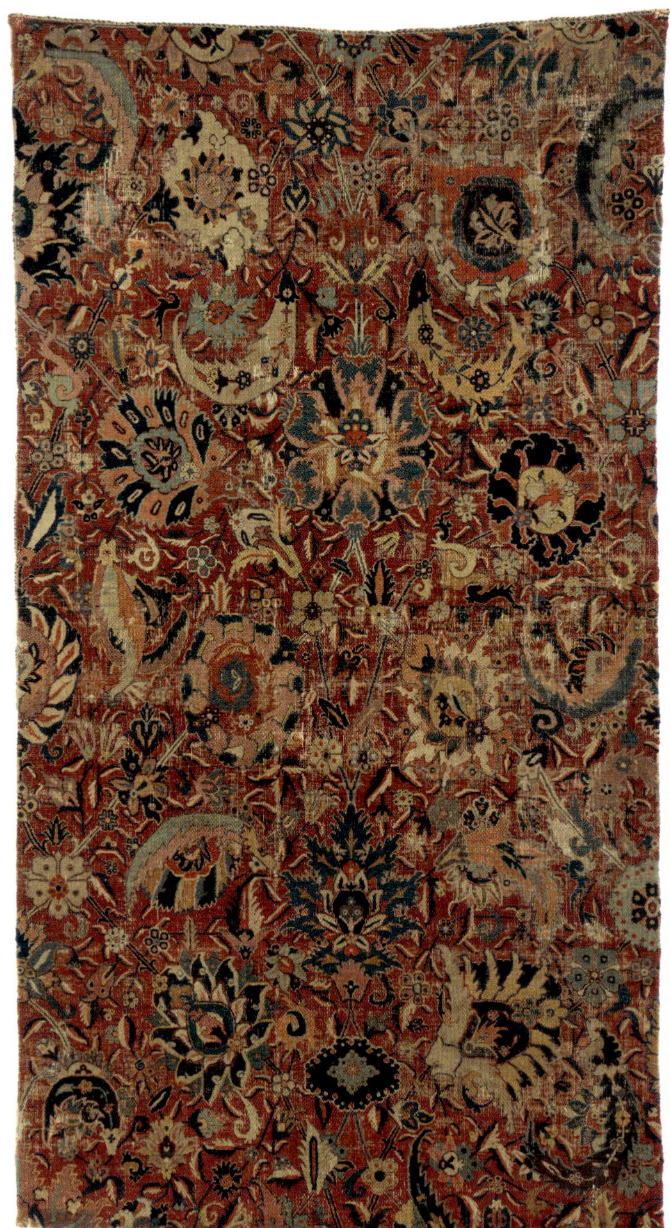

Carpet fragment with three-plane lattice,

Safavid period, about 1600–1700
Made in Kirman, Iran
Cotton warps, wool and cotton wefts; wool pile
215.9 x 116.8 cm
9.10

May H Beattie (1908–97), one of the most distinguished Islamic carpet studies scholars of the twentieth century, surveyed Burrell's carpets in the 1960s and 1970s and wrote about them, including this fragment. With her objectively critical eye, she described it thus: 'This design exemplifies a later stage of the three-plane lattice design. It is so rich in motifs that not only are the floral scrolls as well as the stems difficult to trace, but the whole design has become overcrowded and less well defined.'

Along with another seven pile carpets, two saddlebags, an embroidery and a silk shawl, Burrell bought this fragment in April 1925 at the Brine Baths Hotel in Nantwich, Cheshire, where the carpet dealer Elie Raphael Afoumado (1875–1963) had his gallery, catering for wealthy visitors and collectors.

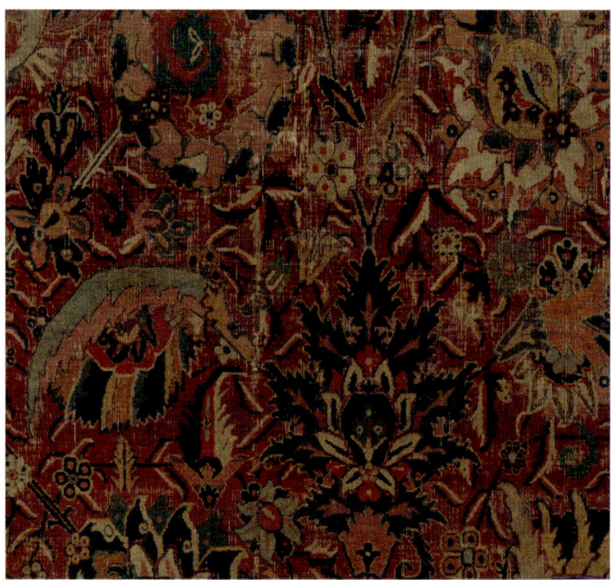

Right: Close inspection reveals that although this carpet fragment at first glance seems to have a generally symmetrical appearance, in fact many of its motifs are not symmetrically placed on the overlapping lattice planes.

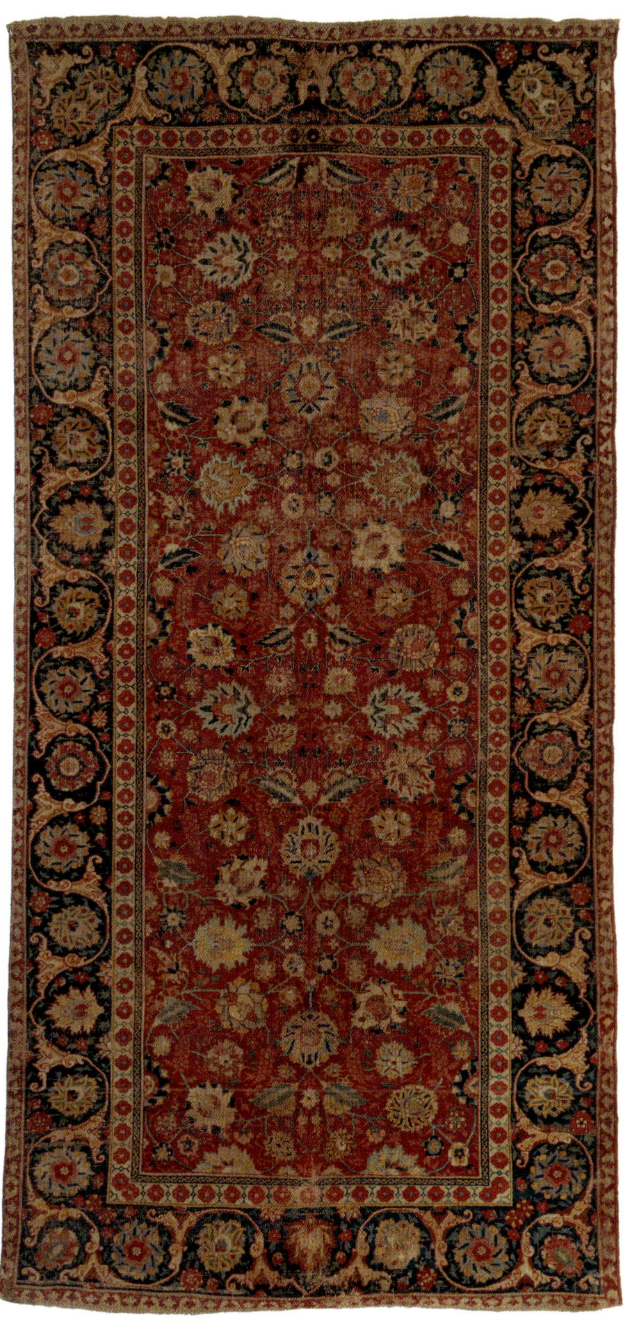

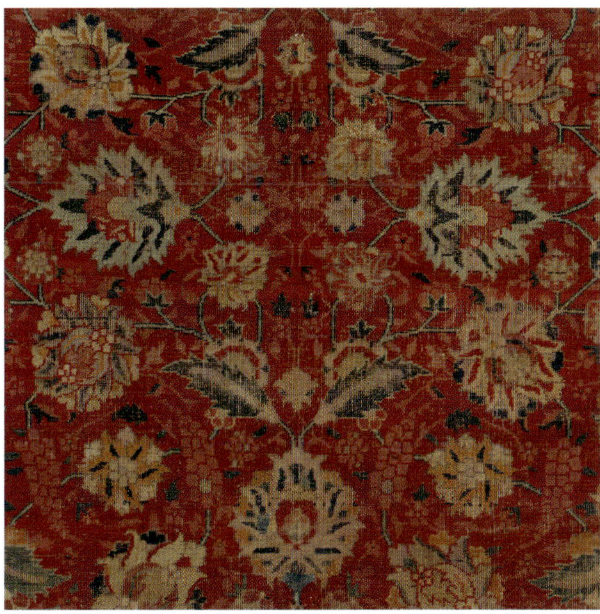

Floral carpet,

Mughal period, about 1600–1700
Made in Lahore, northern India (today in Pakistan)
Cotton warps and wefts; wool pile
345.5 x 157.5 cm
9.33

This Mughal Indian pile carpet follows, in its design and weaving techniques, those made in Iran. Two planes of lattice overlap. The main one, in blue, carries colourful palmettes and pink wisteria-like plumes; the minor one is pale pink and bears small, round flowers, buds and leaves of the same colour.

The top end of the carpet seems to have been extended beyond the natural flow of the repeat pattern originally calculated for it, causing the border pattern to become disrupted at the top corners. Here, the palmettes have been forced to partially merge to accommodate the transition from vertical, along the length of the carpet, to horizontal, along its width. This is caused by a mismatch between the design cartoon and the desired length of the carpet, a not uncommon issue for many handwoven carpets.

Right: This close-up of the field shows how the fine, pale-pink lattice spreads between the palmettes of the bolder, blue lattice.

31

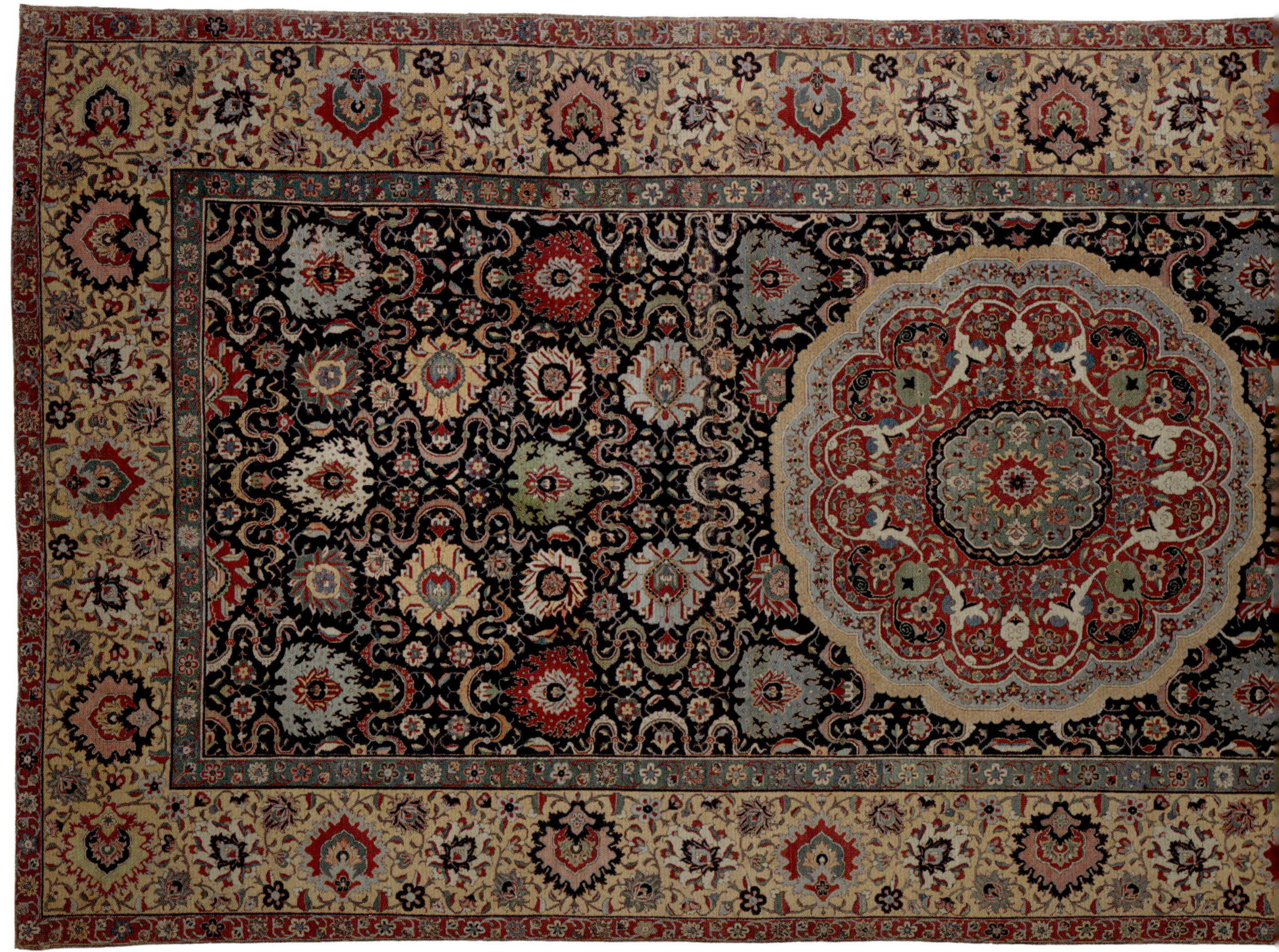

The Dietrichstein carpet,

Safavid period (possibly Qajar), about 1680s–1800
Made in Iran, possibly at Tabriz
Cotton warps and wefts; wool pile
487.7 x 223.6 cm
9.37

A pink medallion, filled with arabesque patterns, sits on a field of arabesque lattice bearing two types of palmettes: conventional ones based on the lotus flower and ones with sharply serrated edges that look like flames, causing these fantastical motifs to be called flaming palmettes. Positioned between these palmettes are elongated, wavy cloud bands that have been borrowed from Chinese art.

The carpet is named after its former owner Prince Alexander Dietrichstein (1899–1964), a member of

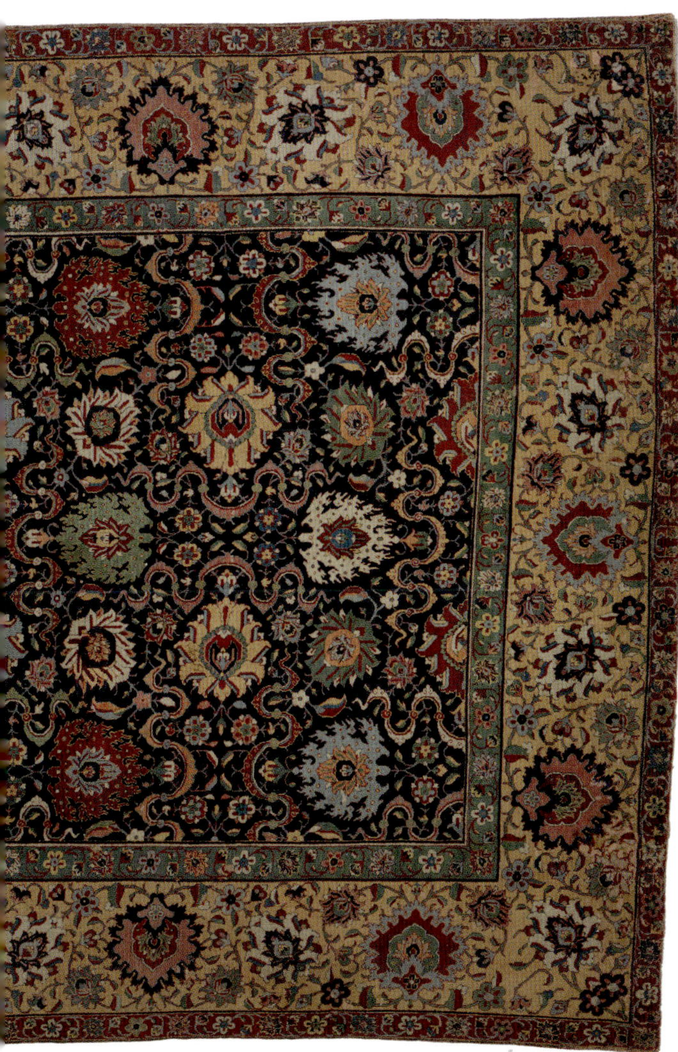

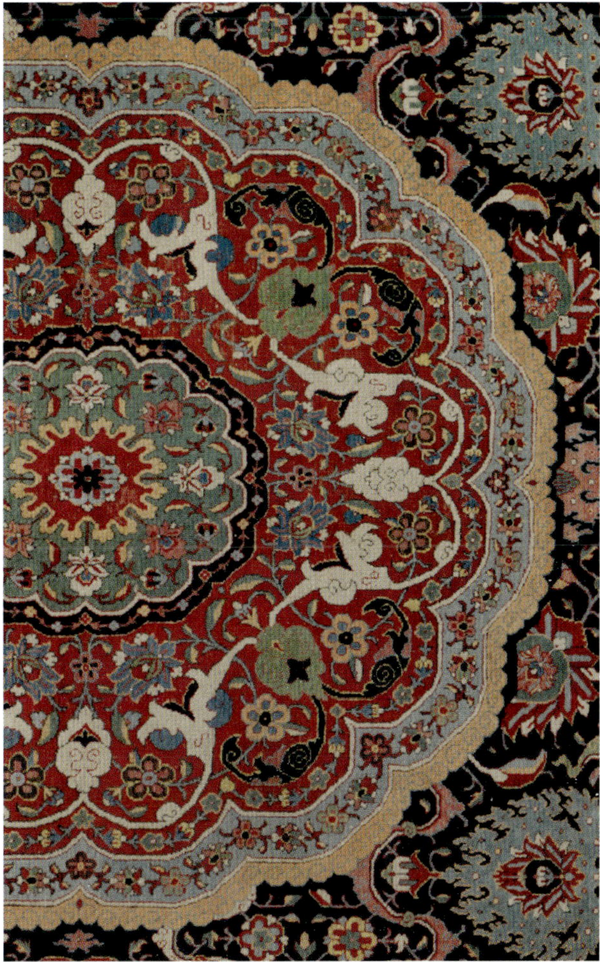

the Bohemian and Austrian Dietrichstein family of Nikolsburg (today known as Mikulov, in the Czech Republic). When he sold it in 1929, he claimed that the carpet had been a gift from the Shah of Iran to the Holy Roman Empress Maria Theresa (1717–80), who in turn gifted it to Prince Alexander's ancestors. Unfortunately, this unverified imperial-relations story is now thought to possibly be mere family lore. But in Burrell's time, in May 1940, it would have played a significant role in the carpet's handsome auction price of £2,000.

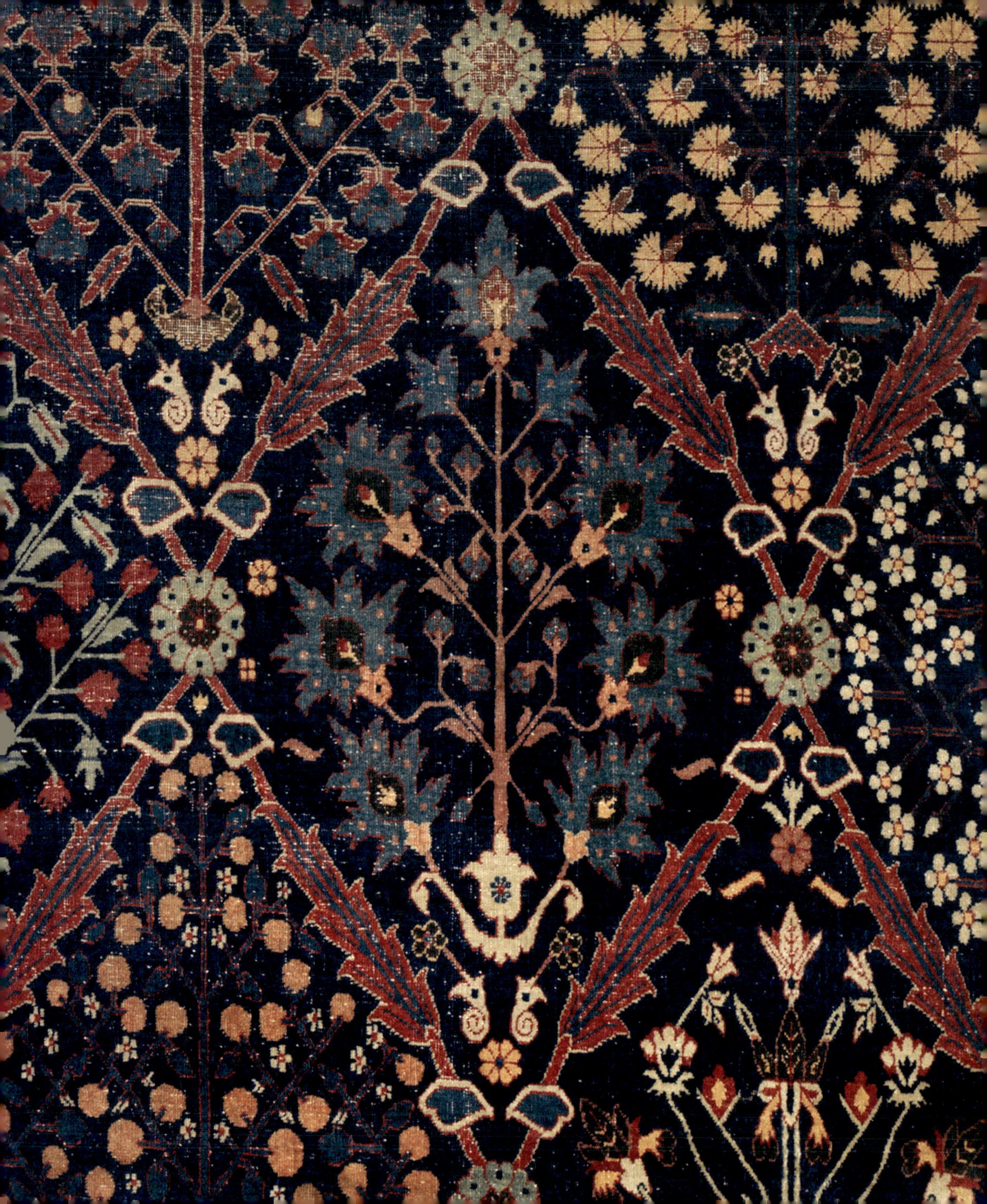

The Persian Carpet

The Burrell Collection holds at least 67 of what, in Europe and North America, are popularly known as Persian carpets. These carpets were woven by peoples in the Iranian sphere of cultural influence, across a large territory that stretched beyond the current boundaries of the modern Iranian state into adjacent parts of the Caucasus and Central Asia. This vast area was historically referred to by Europeans as Persia, a Greek term derived from the ancient Iranian name for the much smaller region that stretches south-west from Isfahan and Kirman to the Persian Gulf. The Burrell Collection's Persian carpets date from the sixteenth to the nineteenth century and have been attributed to a number of important centres of carpet weaving, including the towns of Kirman, Tabriz and Isfahan and the regions of southern, central, western and north-western Iran. They also include examples from the western part of Afghanistan, made in the vicinity of Herat, which was part of the Safavid Empire. The Burrell Persian carpets include ones made in workshops in large urban centres and types made in villages as part of a cottage industry.

Although Persian carpets were sought after in Europe from earlier times, it was during the nineteenth century, particularly in the later decades, that there was a marked rise in the desire to collect early Persian carpets, especially those made in the sixteenth and seventeenth centuries. This heightened interest was caused by an increase in scholarly knowledge in Europe and North America about the cultures and arts of Asia, including the traditions of Iran. These developments then led to a widening of the demand for Persian carpets to include contemporary ones. Carpet and rug dealers, and their agents in the Middle East, sought to satisfy this demand. It was these dealers and agents who enabled connoisseurs of art like Burrell to create their collections of carpets.

Burrell's keenness to secure iconic examples of Persian carpets, especially early ones, led to him not only acquiring fragments, but also accepting heavily repaired and substantially reshaped ones. Out of the 67 Persian carpets in the collection, 25 are fragments of various types and sizes.

While some 30 antique dealers based in the UK, and one in France, helped Burrell build his collection of Islamic carpets, one rug dealership in particular stands out through Sir William's correspondence with Andrew Hannah, the keeper of the Burrell Collection: the London-based Armenian family dealership of A Balian & Son, Importers of Persian Carpets. In addition to selling Burrell at least 21 carpets during the 1930s, they also gave advice on carpet purchases from other dealers and provided a service to repair and clean carpets. At Burrell's request, in 1954 Balian & Son were commissioned by the museums service to update the insurance valuations for all of the Burrell Collection's carpets, in response to steep rises in prices for antique pile carpets sold at auction.

Opposite: This pattern of flowering shrubs set within a diamond-shaped trellis is a fine example of the varied floral designs which are a distinctive feature of Persian carpets. Detail from carpet 9.7 (p. 38).

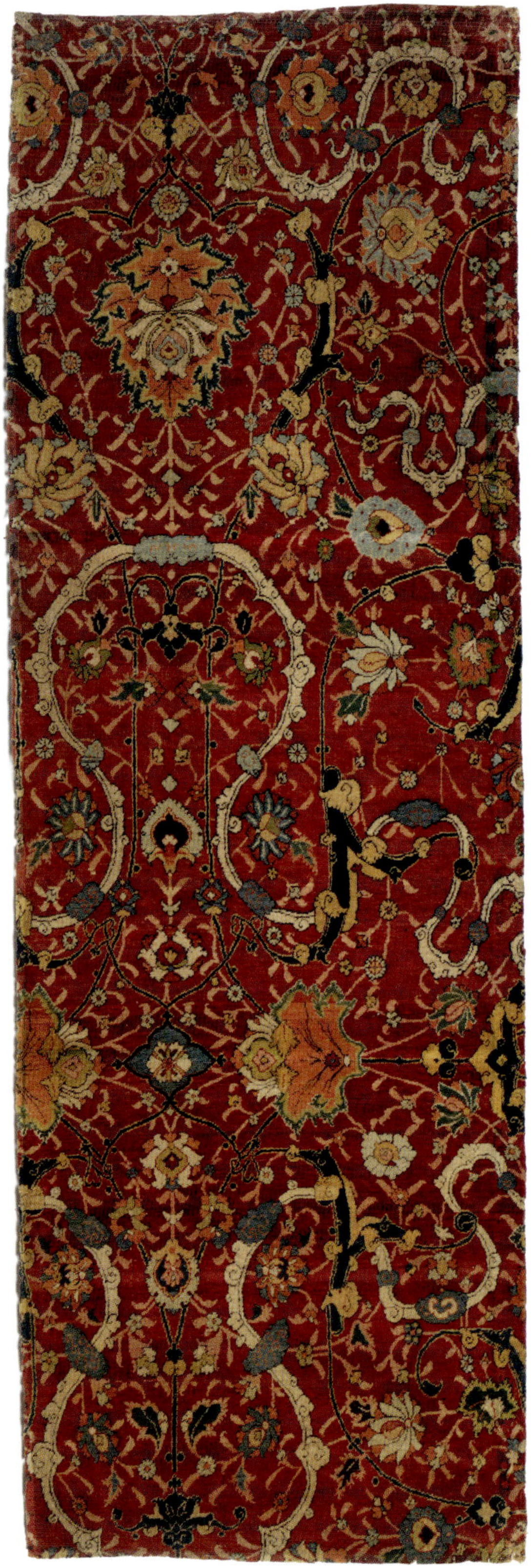

Arabesque carpet fragment with cloud-band design,

Safavid period, late 1500s–early 1600s
Made in Herat, Khurasan region (today in Afghanistan)
Silk warps and wefts; wool pile
157.5 x 61 cm
9.11

Wavy cloud bands inspired by Chinese designs have been added to the two planes of arabesque lattice on this carpet, bringing variety and dynamism to the composition. The original Chinese prototype clouds were first introduced to the Middle East and Central Asia during the Mongol period of rule across these two regions (1256–1353), but by the sixteenth century the appropriation and adaptation of this cloud motif had fully matured into an ornament with a distinct Islamic style, as seen illustrated on this fragment of a very fine Herat carpet.

As for most carpets from the early Safavid period, it has proven hard to pinpoint the exact place where this fragment was woven within the Persian cultural world. When Burrell acquired the piece, it was thought to have been woven in Isfahan, but scholarly revisions of its genre now attribute it to Herat, today in Afghanistan, an equally noteworthy attribution, and even rarer.

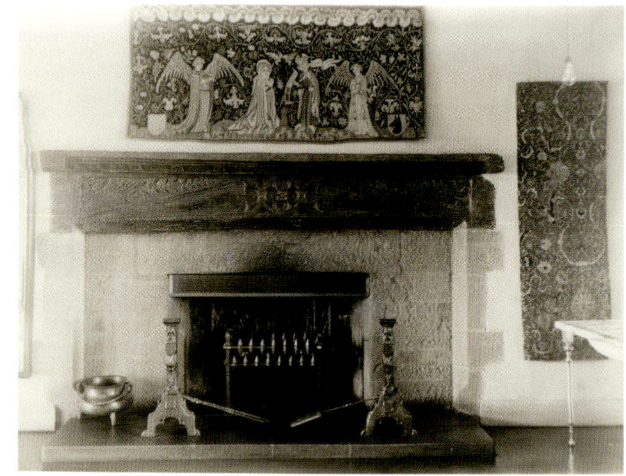

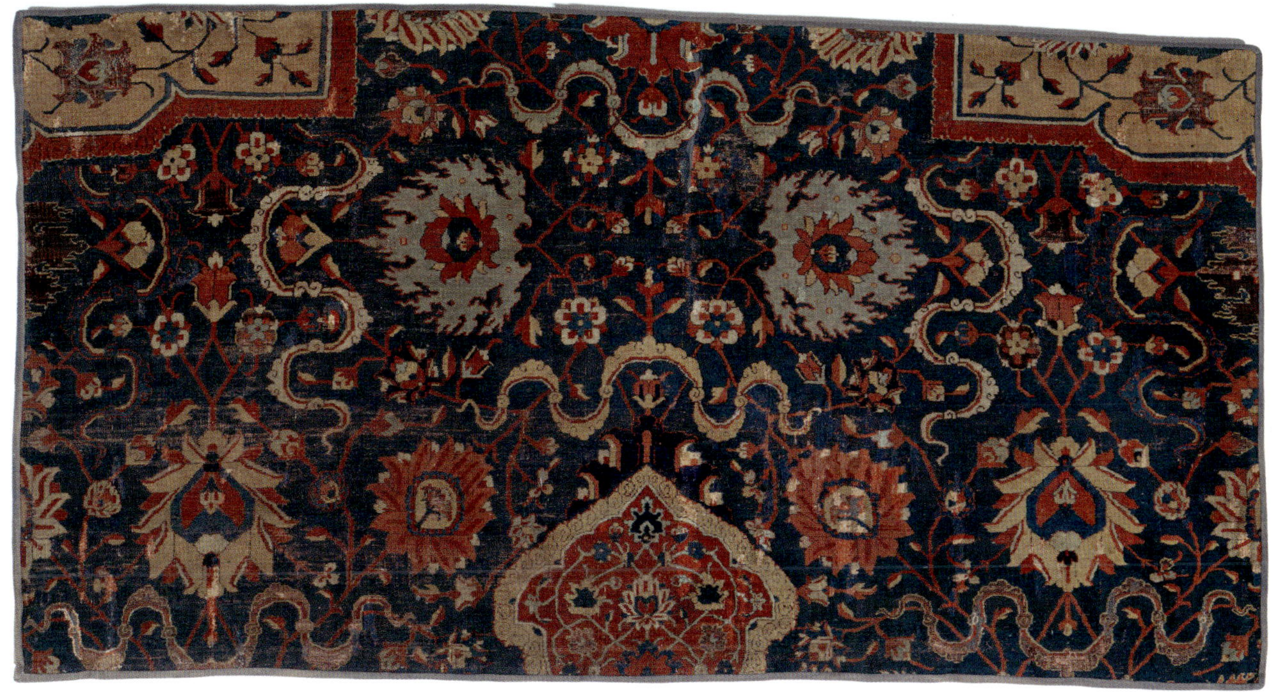

Medallion carpet fragment,

Safavid period, about 1600–1700
Made in Tabriz, Iran
Cotton warps, wool wefts; wool pile
165.3 x 91.5 cm
9.13

This fragment shows a section of the field of a medallion carpet, with part of a red lobed pendant on one of the long sides and parts of two yellow corner pieces on the other. The dark-blue field is occupied by a single lattice of thin, red stems bearing flowers, leaves and palmettes of various designs and sizes. On this lattice are placed wavy cloud bands in several colours – ivory, tan, blue and brown – positioned at right angles in relation to each other. The subtleness of the stem lattice, being deep red on a dark-blue ground, allows the palmettes and the cloud bands to stand out and prevents any impression of overcrowding.

Opposite: In this archival photograph from 1949, carpet fragment 9.11 can be seen hung on the wall to the right of the fireplace in bedroom no. 1 at Hutton Castle. Photograph by Rupert Roddam. Glasgow Museums Archive, GMA.2013.1.1.2467.

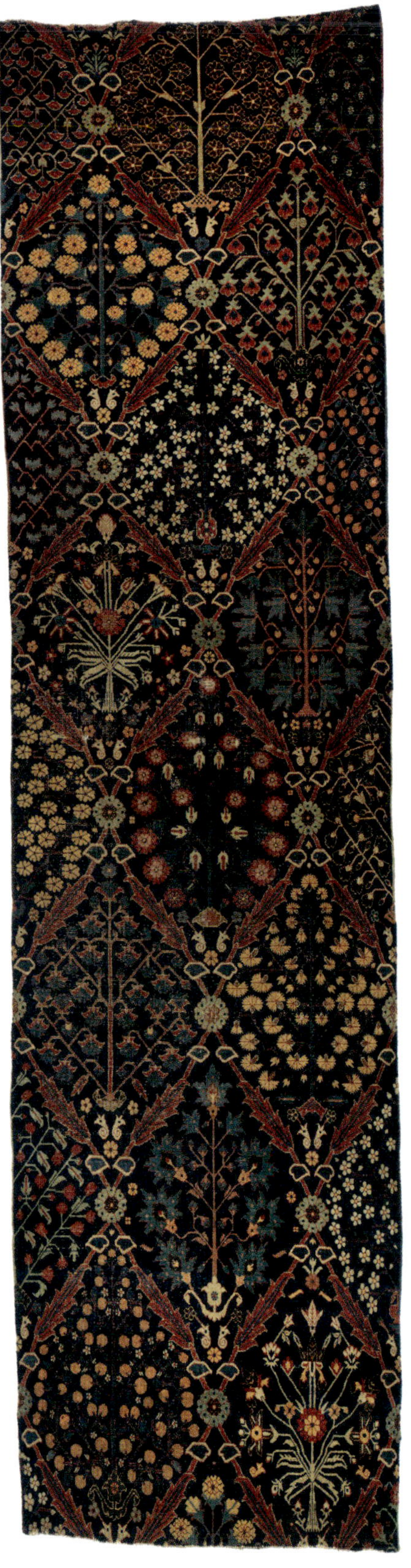

Trellis-design carpet fragment,
Safavid period, about 1600–1700
Made in Kirman, Iran
Cotton warps, wool and cotton wefts; wool pile
398.8 x 101.6 cm
9.7

This carpet is uncommonly long and narrow with no border frame. While it has its full width, with its original selvedges intact, it is missing its top and bottom ends. It is decorated with a single-plane lattice in the shape of a diamond trellis on a dark-blue field. The trellis is made up of long, red serrated leaves linked together by round, yellow flowers. Each diamond-shaped compartment holds a single floral plant. Amongst the flowers represented here are irises, carnations, narcissi, lotuses and roses. These plants are all orientated in the same way, giving the carpet a directional layout. This interesting fact about its structure was pointed out by the dealer when Burrell bought the carpet in 1915, which Burrell noted down in his purchase book.

Herati-pattern carpet,

Qajar period, late 1800s
Made in Hamadan or Ferahan, Kurdish
region, Iran
Cotton warps and wefts; wool pile
322.6 x 170.2 cm
9.115

This is one of a number of later antique
carpets that Burrell acquired in 1925
to furnish his new home at Hutton
Castle. Its type name – Herati-pattern
carpet – relates to the diamond lattice
pattern that occupies the field, which
originated in Herat, Afghanistan,
during the sixteenth century, and was
transferred to western Iran by weavers
from western Afghanistan who were
resettled there in the late 1730s and
1740s during the rule of Nadir Shah
Afshar (1688–1747). This version of
the Herati pattern consists of repeated
diamond-shaped lozenges, each with
a flower in its centre and a palmette
on the outside by each of its points;
sickle-shaped feathery leaves placed
between the palmettes and other
flowers and leaves inserted between
the rows of lozenge patterns complete
the design.

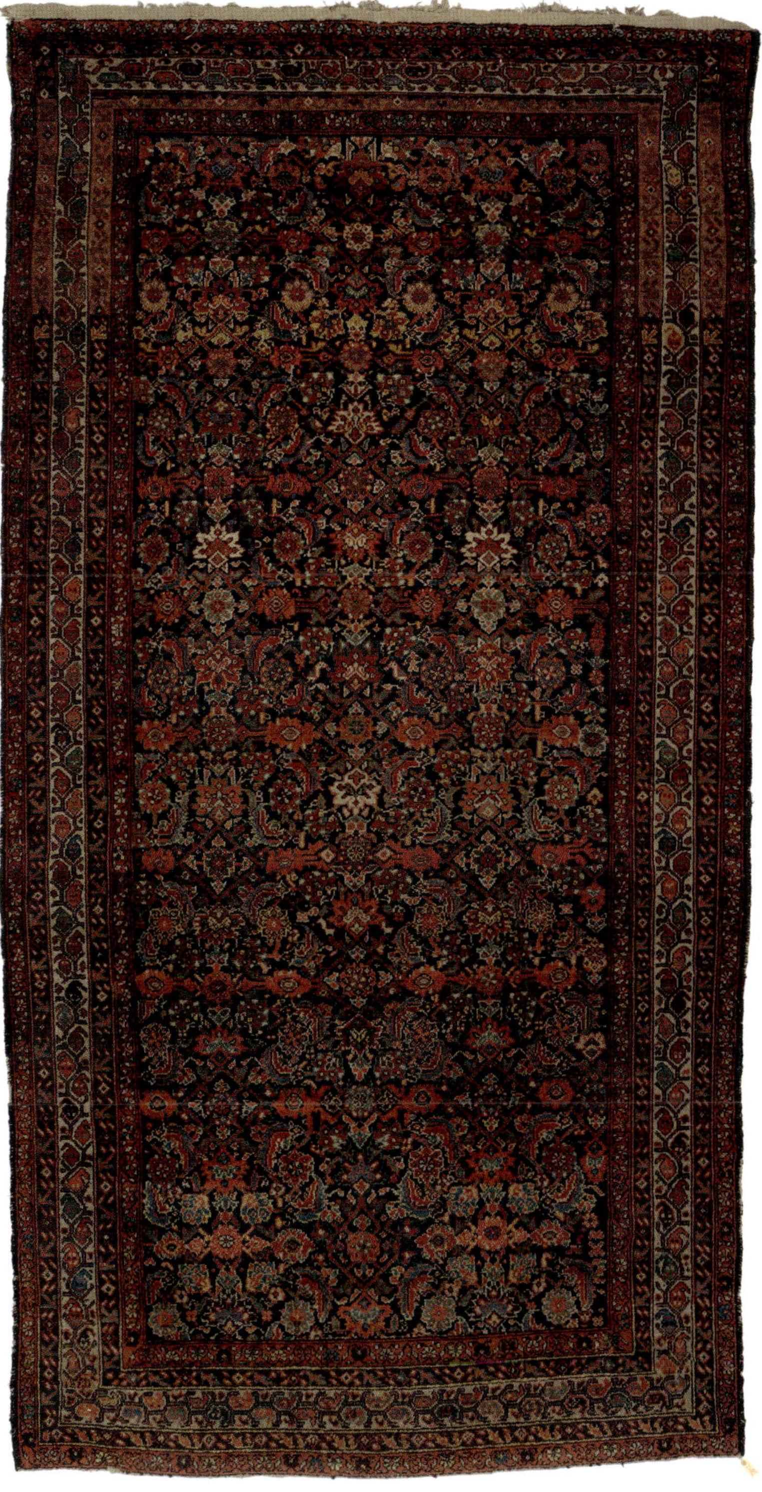

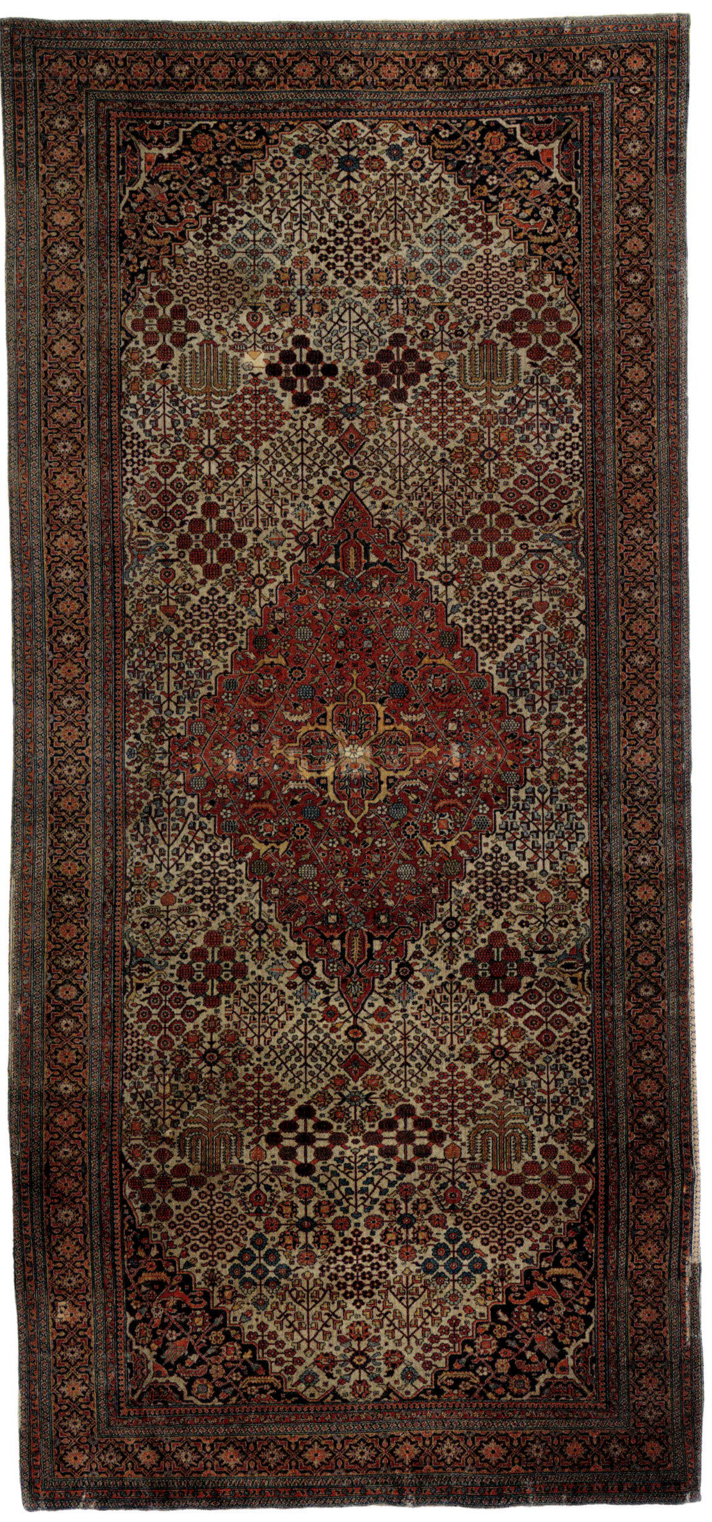

Joshagan carpet,

Qajar period, late 1700s
Made in Jawshaqan (anglicized to Joshagan), Iran
Cotton warps and wefts; wool pile
391.2 x 182.9 cm
9.74

Within the field of this carpet, each lozenge – square in shape but positioned with sides orientated diagonally – holds a flowering plant which is symmetrically formed and shaped to fill and stand alone in its space. In contrast, the diamond-shaped medallion and the four corner pieces of the field are formed of vegetal arabesque patterns. The border complements the geometric design of the field with an arabesque band of eight-pointed stars. This composition evolved in the village of Jawshaqan during the eighteenth century and became its distinguishing design. It was named in the carpet trade as the Joshagan design – an anglicized version of the village's name. This design is still woven there, but it is also now copied and adapted by many other weaving centres in Iran.

Joshagan carpet with diamond design,

Qajar period, early 1800s
Made in Jawshaqan (anglicized to Joshagan),
Iran
Cotton warps and wefts; wool pile
259.1 x 147.3 cm
9.88

A second variation on the Joshagan design
can be seen on this carpet. A blue trellis
creates diamond-shaped lozenges, in each
of which is placed a flowering plant. These
motifs are very similar in shape and size but
differ in the shape of their petals and their
colours. They are repeated in a staggered
arrangement that creates diagonal rows of
each motif.

This carpet once belonged to the Glasgow-
based carpet manufacturers James Templeton
& Co. (1839–1974). In the early twentieth
century the company collected Persian pile
carpets to use as prototypes to aid in the
design of its machine-made carpets. The
photographic albums of Templeton's collection,
in which this carpet is featured, are now in
the University of Glasgow Archives.

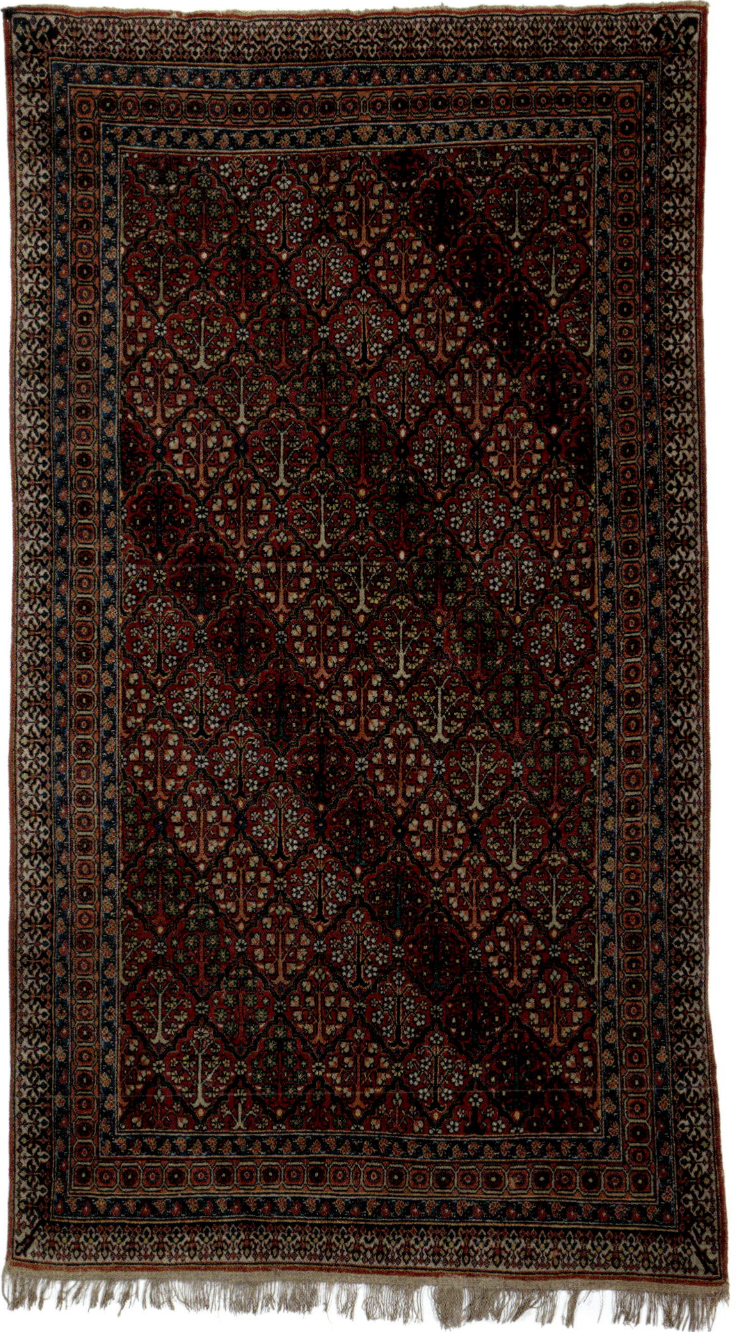

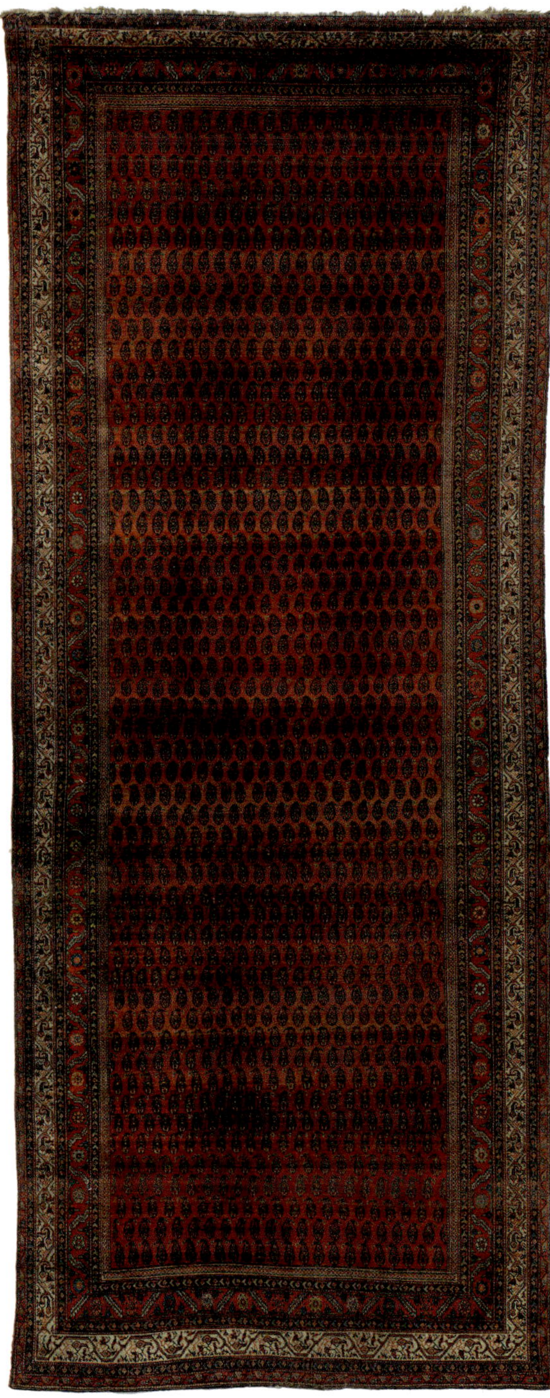

Seraband carpet,

Qajar period, about 1800–1900
Made in the Ser-e Band (anglicized to Seraband)
district, Iran
Cotton warps and wefts; wool pile
594.3 x 231.2 cm
9.81

Delicate, dark-blue-outlined *boteh* motifs, in offset rows, fill the field of this carpet. The *boteh* – popularly known in the United Kingdom from the mid nineteenth century as the Paisley pattern – is an almond-shaped motif with a bent tip, which is filled with a floral or leaf pattern. The border's light-coloured frame with its red-and-blue vine scroll is a distinguishing feature of this type of carpet.

Seraband carpets were a commercial product, woven in large numbers and impressive sizes. The subtle *boteh* motif on them is thought to have been borrowed from printed Indian cotton textiles of the eighteenth century. Burrell acquired six Seraband carpets to furnish his home (one can be seen in the photograph of the hall at Hutton Castle on p. 6, in the left foreground). Although they look very similar in layout and colour combination, none share identical *botehs*.

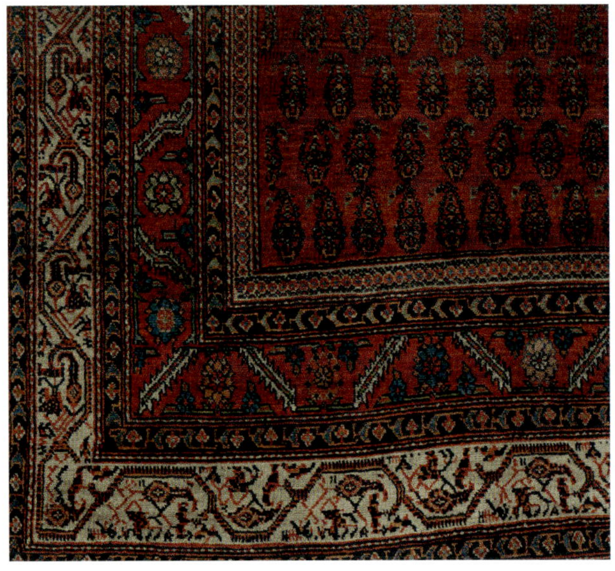

Right: The border of this carpet is strikingly intricate, made up of several frames and a number of single-knot lines of various colours. Each frame has a floral scroll, and the white frame – typical of Seraband carpets – provides an effective contrast to the others.

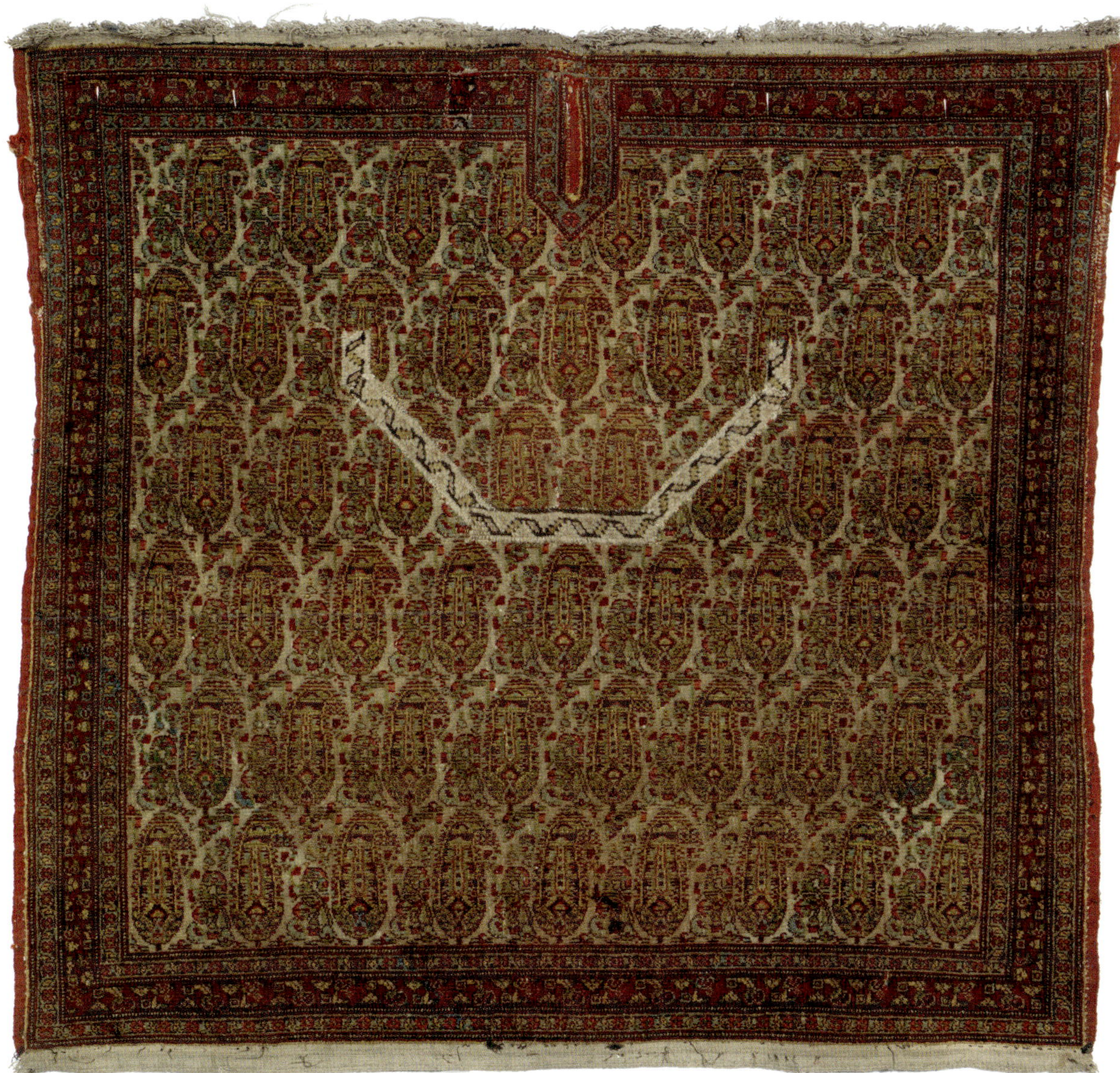

Cover for a horse saddle,

Qajar period, mid 1800s
Made in Senneh (today Sanandaj), Kurdish region,
Iran
Wool warps and wefts; wool pile
104 x 101 cm
9.125

This saddle cover was woven using the knotted-pile technique of carpet making. Two openings were woven into the cover: a small vertical one on the top edge, to accommodate the pommel at the front of the saddle, and a curved slit in the centre, to accommodate the cantle at the back of the saddle. These openings have since been sealed to allow the cover to be used for other purposes.

The cover's decorative scheme consists of offset rows of the *boteh* motif. Seven colours have been used to create the delicate *botehs* and the little flowers that surround them. The colours of these motifs are best appreciated on the reverse side of the cover, where they have escaped the fading effects of the sun.

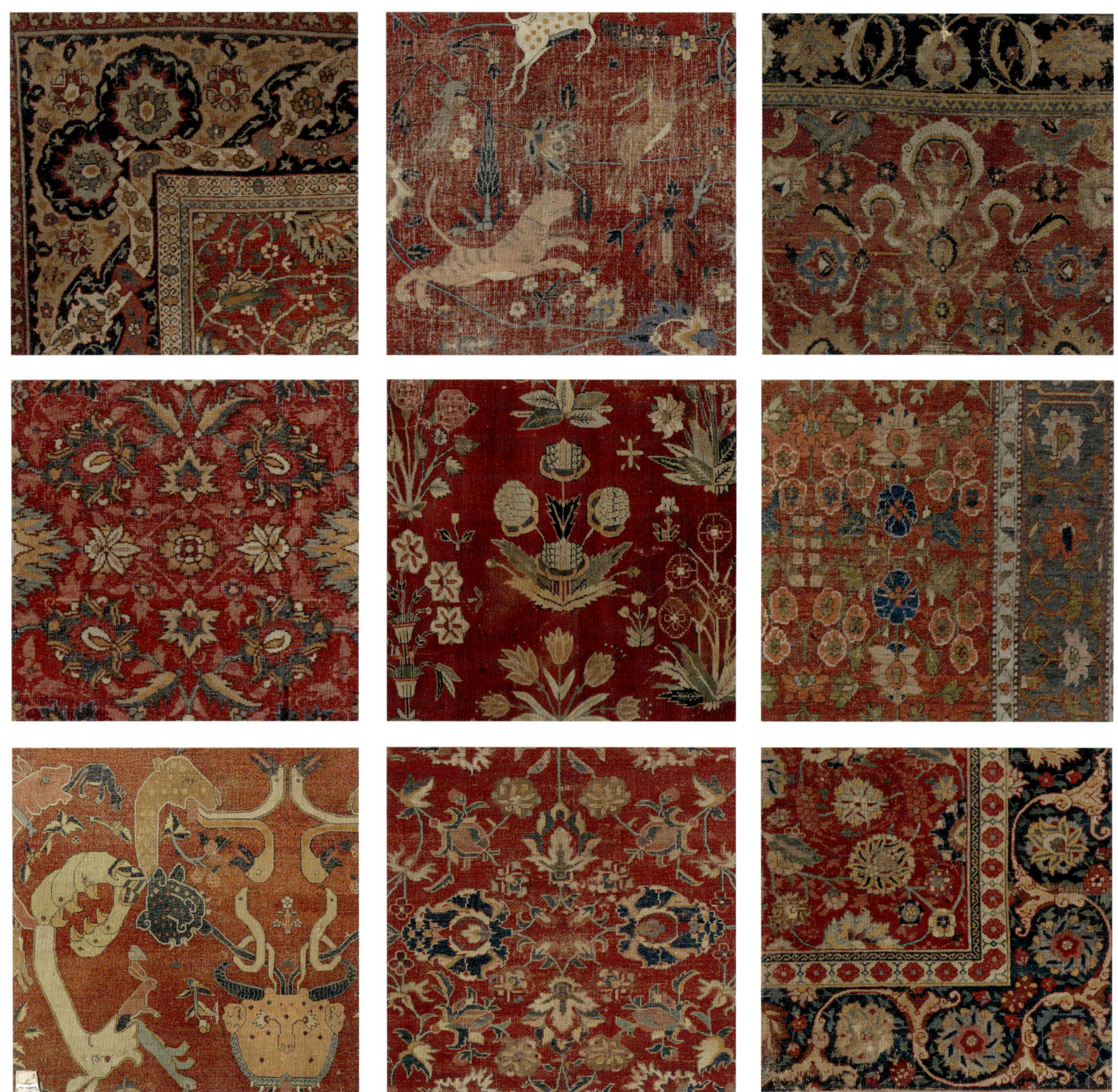

The Mughal Indian carpets in the collection are in a wide range of
design styles, from arabesque to naturalistic.
Top row: details from carpets 9.34, 9.32 (pp. 54–55), 9.26 (p. 46).
Middle row: details from carpets 9.29 (p. 47), 9.12 (p. 48), 9.87 (p. 49).
Bottom row: detail from the back of carpet 9.1 (pp. 52–53), details from carpets 9.35, 9.33 (p. 31).

Mughal India's Carpet Tradition

Although pile-carpet weaving is an ancient tradition in many parts of Asia, with archaeological excavations revealing examples that go back to at least 500 BC, the tradition in the Indian subcontinent is comparatively recent, introduced to the region in the sixteenth century by the Mughal Dynasty (1526–1857). The origins of this Indian carpet tradition lie in the Persian carpet world, where the Mughals' Turkic cultural preferences and ethnic roots rest. The courts of the Safavids in Iran and the Mughals in India were also engaged in a Persianate cultural dialogue, with the Mughals emulating the Safavids in many aspects of their courtly life, and the Persian language – known to native speakers as Farsi – being adopted as the official and the literary and poetic language of their court in India.

During the reigns of the first five Mughal emperors – Babur, Humayun, Akbar, Jahangir and Shah Jahan, who in succession ruled between 1526 and 1657 – Iranian and Afghan artists and master craftsmen were encouraged to settle in northern India, especially in the three capital cities of Lahore, Agra and Fatehpur Sikri. They staffed the royal workshops and trained local artisans and craftsmen in a range of the arts, from miniature painting and manuscript illumination to pile-carpet weaving.

Through this combination of circumstances, Indian pile carpets came to reflect court style in subject matter, aesthetics and techniques. This was made possible by an organized close collaboration between the designers and weavers of the royal workshops.

Early examples of their collaborations have, by Europeans, been termed 'Indo-Persian' and 'Indo-Isfahan' – Isfahan being a distinguished centre of Safavid carpet weaving in Iran – because of the marked resemblance between them and their Persian prototypes.

During the reign of Emperor Akbar, from 1556 to 1605, there emerged a distinctly Mughal tradition in the visual arts, including in carpet design, which favoured naturalistic depictions of the flora and fauna of the subcontinent and incorporated the iconography and aesthetics of the native arts of India.

During the 1930s Burrell purchased a dozen Indian pile carpets made during the sixteenth and seventeenth centuries. They include several with variations on the Persian-influenced vegetal arabesque design (such as carpet 9.33, p. 31), one with a naturalistic floral design (carpet 9.12, p. 48) and two wild-animal carpets (carpet 9.1, pp. 52–53, and carpet 9.32, pp. 54–55).

But Burrell's interest in India was not confined to collecting carpets. In the autumn of 1922 he and his family set off on a wide tour of India that lasted until the spring of 1923 and included visits to Jaipur and Delhi amongst many other locations. Burrell's library also illustrates his interest. Amongst its titles that relate to the history and arts of various parts of the Islamic world, there are a number about India, from a biography of Emperor Babur, to several volumes concerning the history of the British presence in India, to European creative works inspired by Indian culture, such as the Mughal-inspired poetic romance *Lalla Rookh*, first published in 1817, by the Irish writer Thomas Moore (1779–1852).

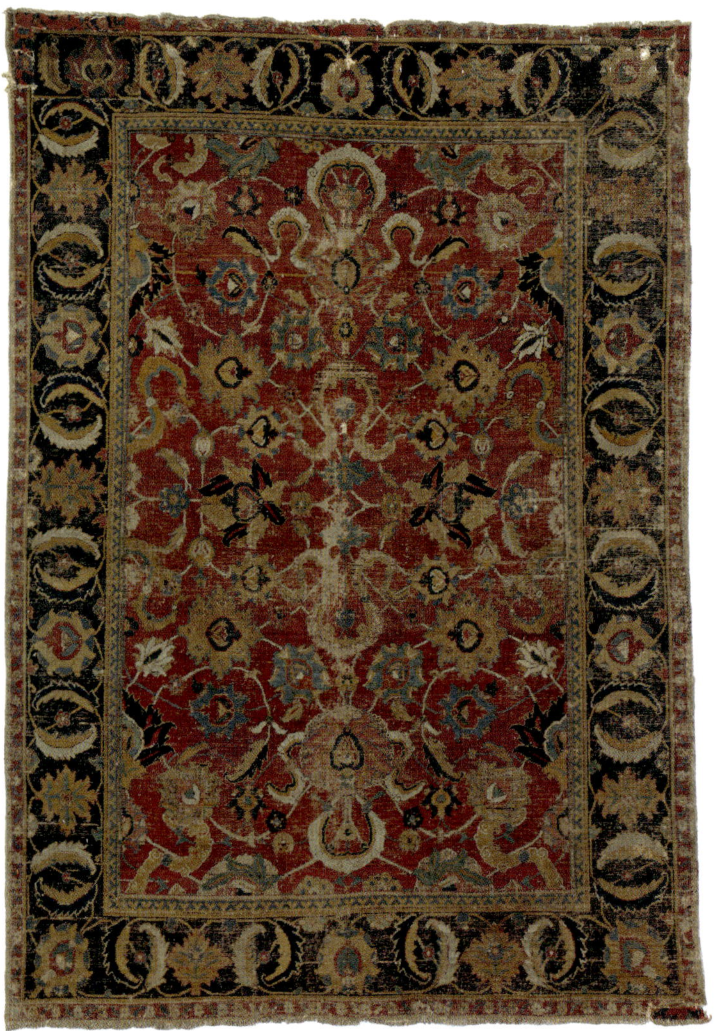

Indo-Isfahan carpet,

Mughal period, late 1600s
Made in northern India, possibly at Agra
Cotton warps and wefts; wool pile
205.8 x 142.2 cm
9.26

The classical Indo-Isfahan style is represented by this carpet. Like its Persian counterparts, its design consists of two overlapping vegetal lattices bearing palmettes, flowers and serrated leaves. The main plane has white stems and the secondary one has blue stems. Intertwined with them are curly cloud bands in three different colours: white, ochre-yellow and brown. The pile dyed with the brown colour has badly disintegrated, totally exposing the warps and the wefts. Other motifs where this brown yarn has been used have also suffered in a similar manner.

Three shades of dark blue have been used in the field and the border. The darkest blue, almost black in appearance, can be seen in the leaves of some of the field's palmettes. Such a depth of blue is achieved by the repeated dipping of woollen yarn in indigo dye – the more dips, the darker the yarn becomes.

Floral carpet,

Mughal period, late 1600s
Made in Lahore, northern India (today in Pakistan)
Cotton warps and wefts; wool pile
401.3 x 193 cm
9.29

Both the red field and the dark-blue border of this carpet are intricately filled with colourful motifs. In both there are two planes of decoration. In the field there is a blue stem lattice carrying an array of colourful palmettes and flowers; beneath it is a delicate pink lattice, with simpler floral motifs, which meanders in the spaces left clear by the blue stem lattice. In the border a yellow stem scroll carries palmettes and serrated leaves, and a pale-blue leaf scroll spreads in the background.

This tone-on-tone use of colours – pink on red and light blue on dark blue, with no outlines separating the lighter colours from the colours of the backgrounds – is a defining feature of Mughal Lahore carpets of the seventeenth century (see also carpet 9.33, p. 31).

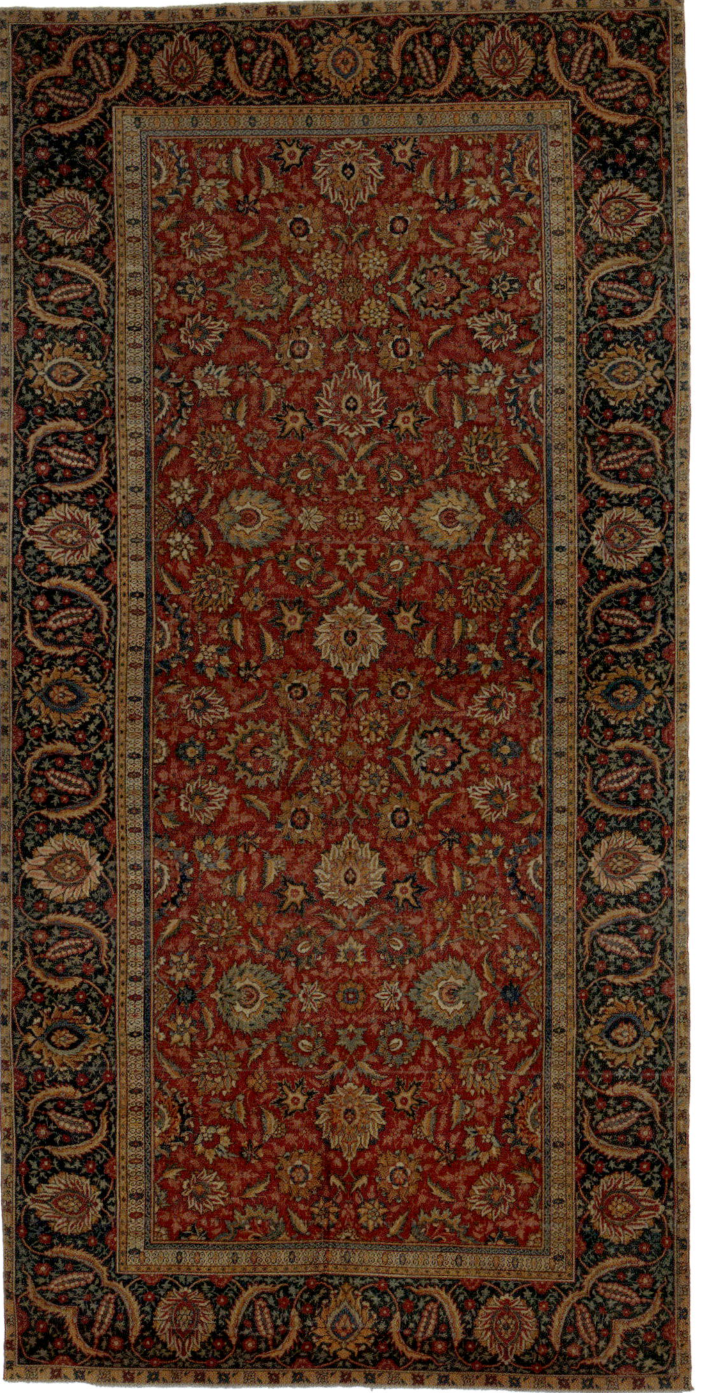

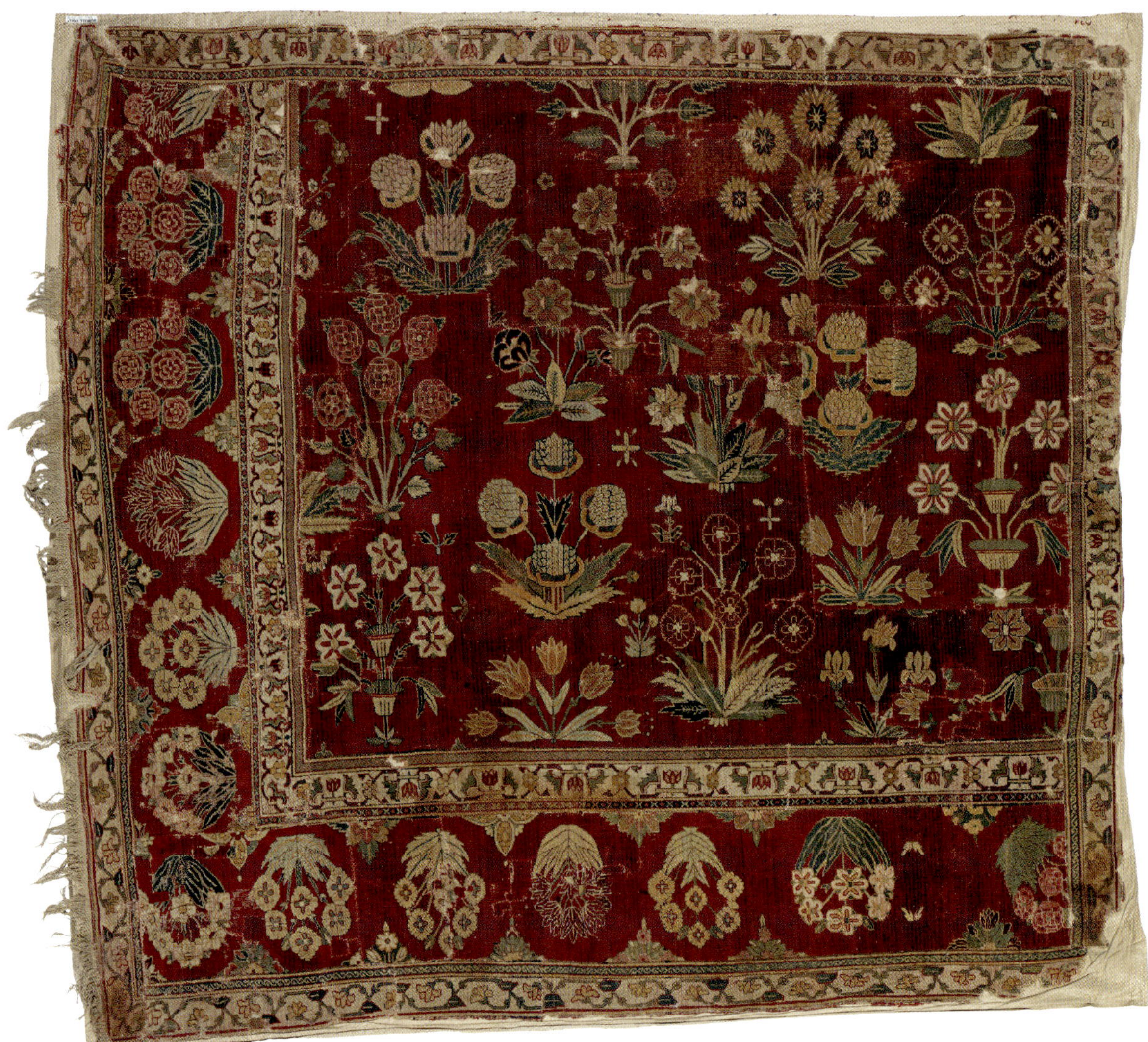

Amber Palace carpet fragment,

Mughal period, about 1652–54
Made in northern India
Cotton warps, cotton and silk wefts; wool pile
190.5 x 180.3 cm
9.12

Several fragmentary parts of the field and border of a large carpet have been put together in this piece. Its floral design scheme represents the naturalistic style of Mughal painting, from which the motifs have been borrowed. Red carnations and tulips, yellow lilies and irises, and pink roses are amongst the variety of flowers represented here. This composite fragment comes from a carpet once owned by Raja Jai Singh I (1611–67), a Hindu Rajput prince and the ruler of the Kingdom of Amber (the 'b' in Amber is silent), who had a distinguished military career under the Mughal emperor Shah Jahan (1592–1666). Scholarly research into Jai Singh's carpets reveal that the carpet was purchased for him in Lahore in 1654 and used at his palace at Amber.

Mughal 'millefleurs' carpet,

Mughal period, about 1800–1900
Made in northern India
Cotton warps, cotton and wool wefts; wool pile
449.6 cm x 292.1 cm
9.87

Narrow bands of a floral lattice are horizontally repeated to fill the red field of this carpet. Each lattice band has green stems and leaves, and flowers in a variety of colours – blue, salmon pink, pale pink, ivory and orange. These lattice bands are complemented by the red field's *abrash* colour variation (*abrash* is a Persian term for mixed shades of colour, which when describing carpets refers to striations), where differences in the tones of batches of red-dyed yarn are employed to create horizontal bands of colour in subtle gradation.

Millefleurs – 'a thousand flowers' in French – is a European designation for this type of Mughal-period repeat pattern of small flowers, almost always naturalistically depicted. The design is a development on the Herati pattern (for an example, see carpet 9.115, p. 39).

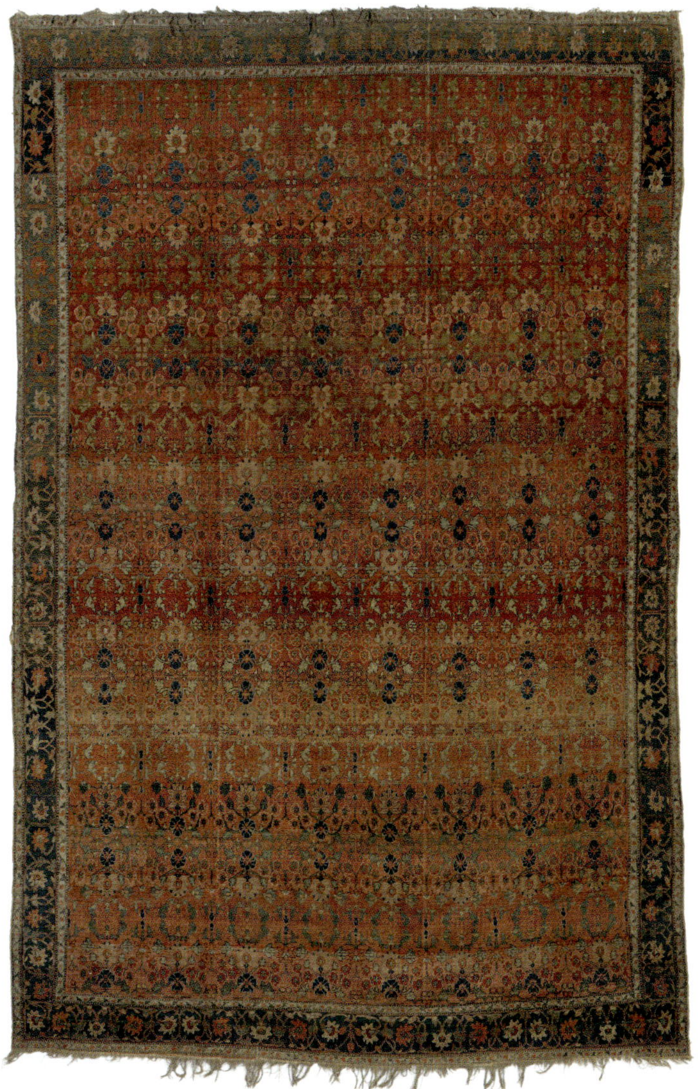

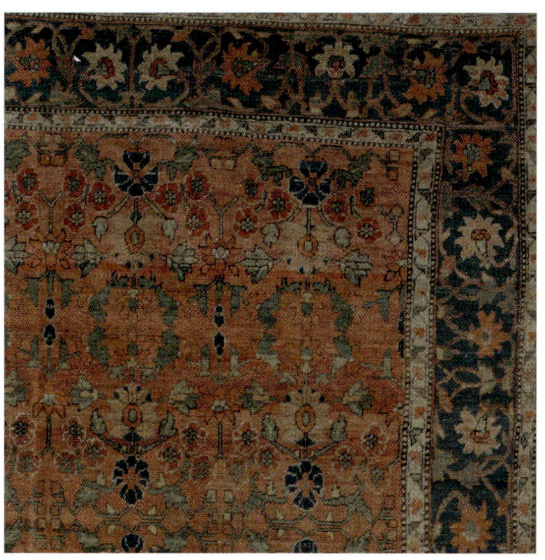

This carpet has naturalistic flowers in the field and border, and striations of different tones of red in the field.

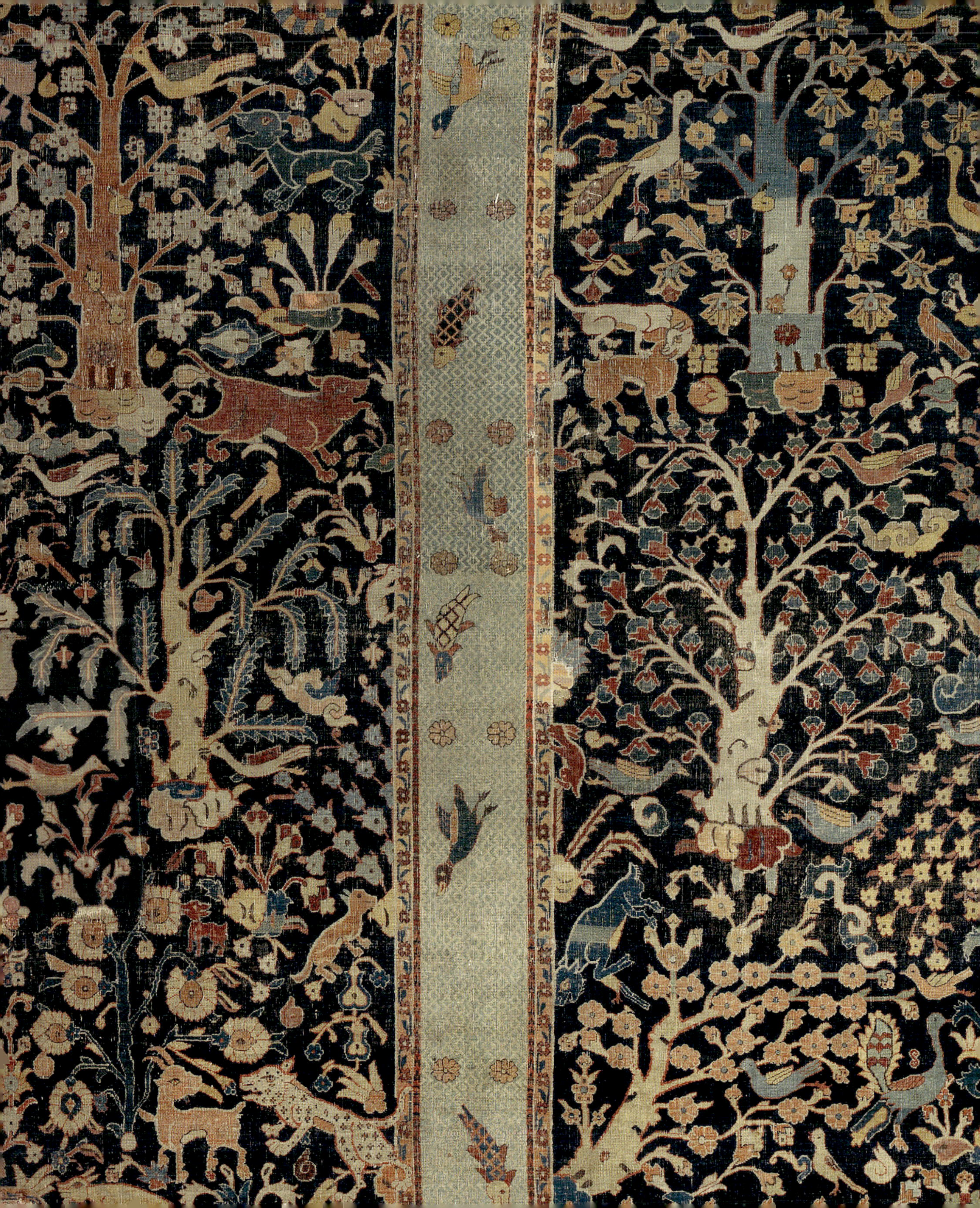

Animals in Carpets: Naturalistic and Imaginary

Fifteen carpets in the collection have animals and birds depicted on them. Some of these are prominently illustrated as part of the design theme, as can be seen on the Wagner garden carpet (carpet 9.2, pp. 18–21 and opposite). Others are subtly or discreetly inserted amongst motifs that make up the main design. While some of the animals are realistically depicted, others are simplified in shape, though still distinguishable; others are abstracted to such an extent that a little bit of imagination is needed to spot them. Only three of the Burrell carpets contain imaginary creatures. These include dragons (carpet 9.38, pp. 58–59) and the heads of demons (carpet 9.1, pp. 52–53).

The presence of all these types of creatures may puzzle some, especially those who have formed an impression that figurative depictions and imagery are prohibited by the Islamic faith, and therefore assume that Islamic art is devoid of them. However, the realities of Islamic material heritage and culture witness to the contrary, as is illustrated by the many Islamic objects in the Burrell Collection that feature figurative decoration, which come from different parts of the world and historical periods, and include metals, ceramics and a variety of textiles including carpets.

Animals were an integral part of people's lives, both those domesticated and those in the surrounding wilderness. The importance of animals and interaction with them has been expressed through oral traditions, in literature and through material culture. The depiction of animals on objects reflects their influential presence and the symbolism and metaphors it inspired. It ought not to be surprising to see wild animals appearing on Mughal carpets (such as carpets 9.1, pp. 52–53, and 9.32, pp. 54–55), if we reflect that the Mughal emperors were fond of collecting exotic animals in their royal menageries, that they hunted game of all kinds as a sport, and that they paraded animals which symbolized nobility, power and authority as part of their daily court activities. These carpets would have fitted into and complemented the cultural scene that played out around them.

Opposite: This carpet has been created by a designer whose observations of the natural world enabled him to charmingly populate its garden and its waterways with a variety of animals, birds, insects and fish, with some creatures in predator and prey compositions. Detail from carpet 9.2 (pp. 18–21).

Object in Focus

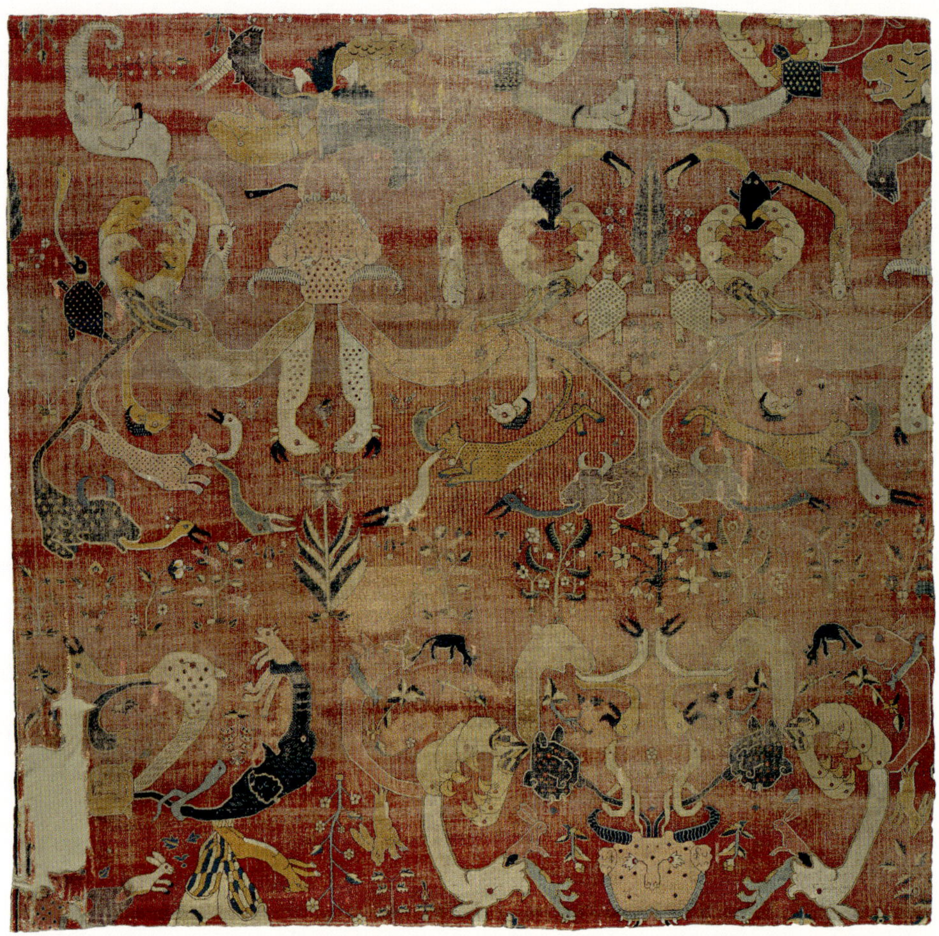

This fragment once formed part of the field of one of a pair of carpets that measured approximately twenty metres long by four metres wide. The pair were made for the audience hall of the Mughal emperor Akbar (1542–1605).

Here, wild animals and birds of the Indian subcontinent leap out of each other's mouths in a chain of fantastical compositions. The range of beasts is extensive and includes the heads of elephants, rhinoceroses, camels, nilgai antelopes, blackbuck antelopes, tigers, lions, a leopard, black panthers, oxen, onagers (Asiatic wild asses found in parts of northern India), rabbits and hares, snakes, geese, black-necked storks, parrots, peacocks, fish and crocodile-like beasts, and the whole figures of cheetahs, turtles, hyenas and dog- and monkey-like quadrupeds.

These chains of animals and birds are connected to two different demonic heads with horns – the only supernatural creatures present on the carpet – from which the animal chains seem to emerge. The positioning of the demonic heads resembles the positioning of large palmettes or vases in vegetal arabesque compositions, from which lattices of stems emerge and spread.

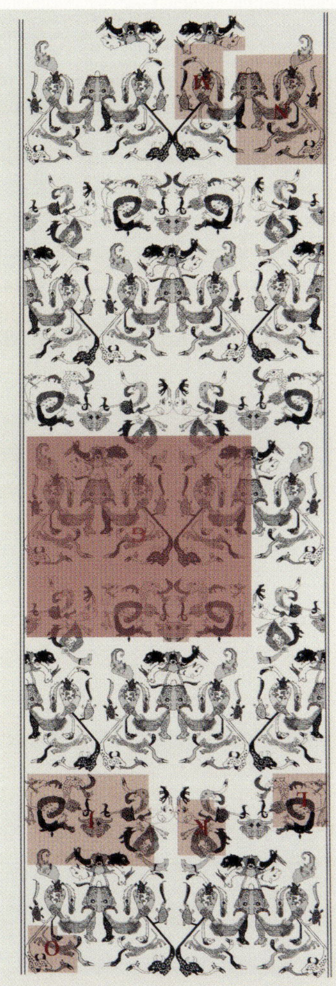

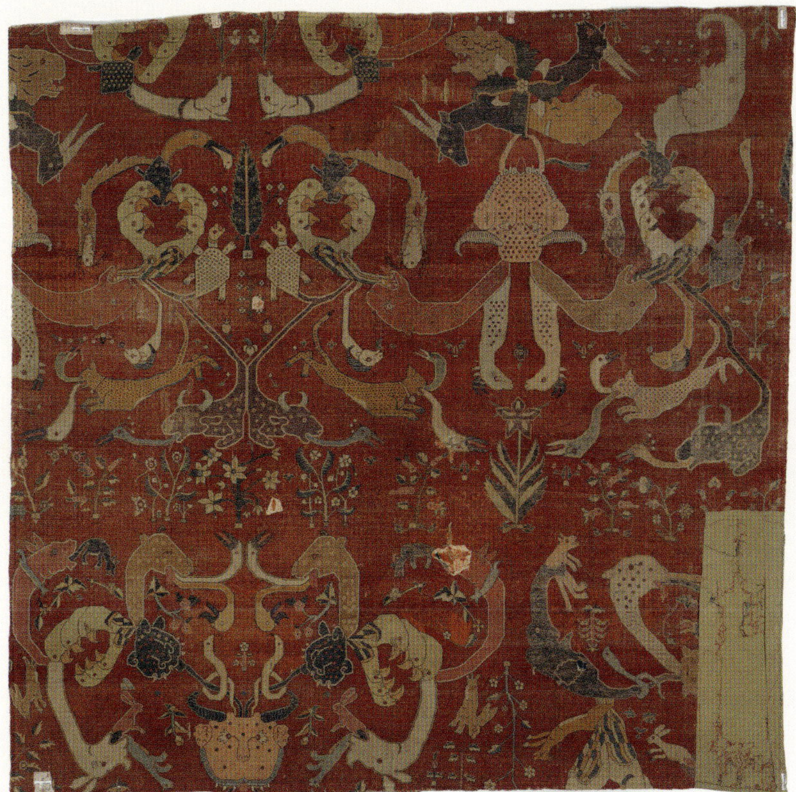

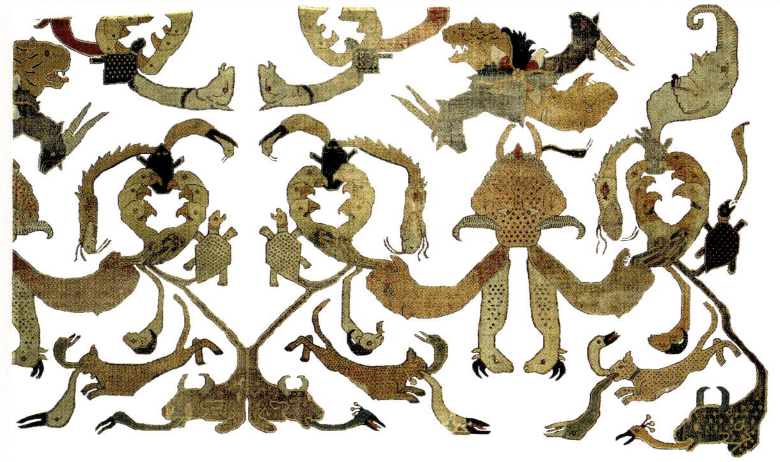

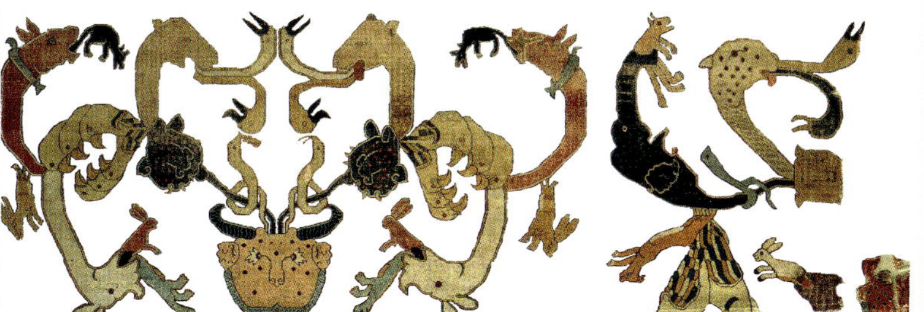

Above: This diagram shows the extent of the original whole carpet and the position within it of the Burrell fragment, represented by the largest and darkest pink shaded area. From *Silk and Stone: The Art of Asia*, Hali Publications, 1996, in the chapter 'A Fearful Symmetry, The Mughal Red-Ground "Grotesque" Carpets' by Steven J Cohen (with darkening to the largest shaded area added).

Above, right: In this image of the back of the carpet, the colour of the field and the floral motifs have been removed, allowing the animal compositions to be seen more easily.

Right: In this image of the back of the carpet, the red ground of the field and the floral motifs have been removed, allowing the animal compositions to be seen more easily.

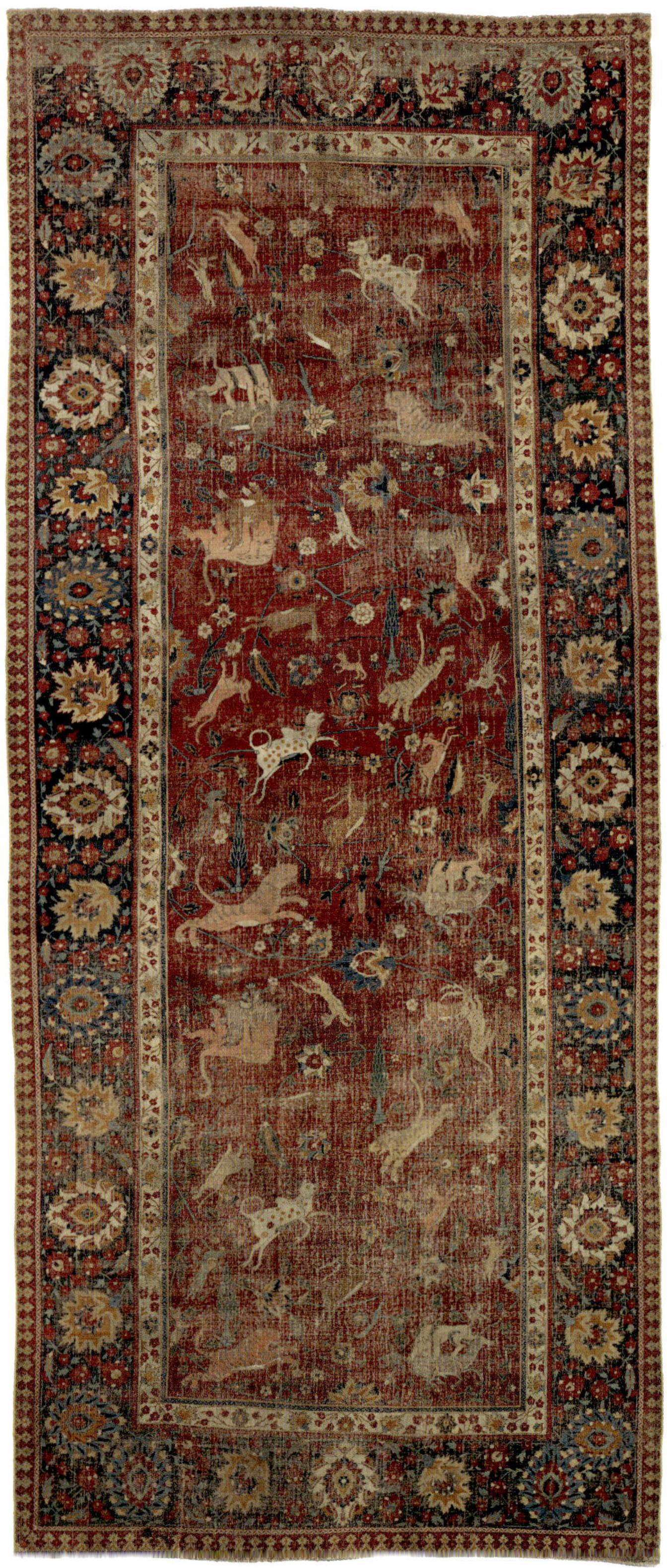

Mughal animal carpet,

Mughal period, about 1600–1700
Made in Lahore, northern India (today in Pakistan)
Cotton warps and wefts; wool pile
475 x 200.7 cm
9.32

This design is full of wild animals of the Indian jungle: tigers pouncing, hump-backed cattle frolicking, gazelles sprinting, lions attacking antelope and devouring bears, hares hopping and a number of small quadrupeds running around. Also present are blue parrots and white cockatoos.

But notice the two cheetahs – each has pinned down a deer. These cheetahs are not wild, for they are wearing collars – a tell-tale sign that they are hunting cheetahs, reared especially for this purpose, and considered prized companions of royal hunting parties. The cheetahs on carpet 9.1 (pp. 52–53) are also hunting animals.

The designers of this carpet cleverly used the asymmetrical repeat pattern to evoke a real wilderness in which animals might live. It is unfortunate that some parts of this carpet have suffered from a considerable loss of surface pile due to heavy use. This loss makes it harder to appreciate the full charm of some of the animal depictions, such as the bears that are being attacked by lions and the hunting cheetahs.

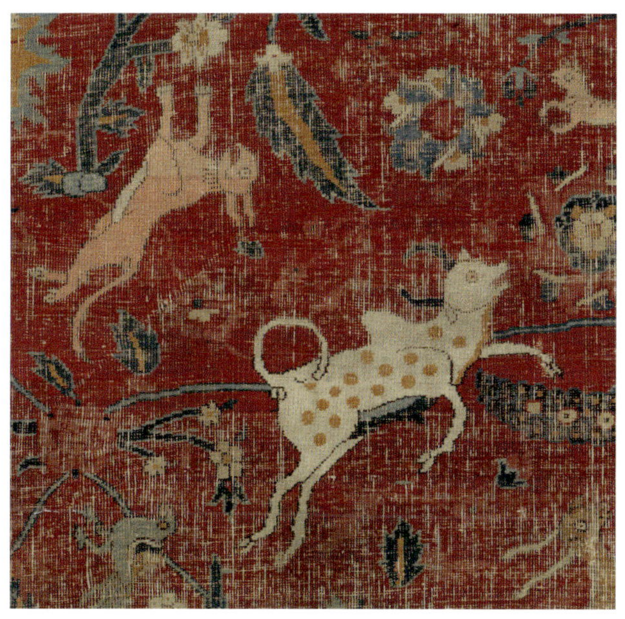

A white-humped cow with yellow spots and a pink hare run across the field.

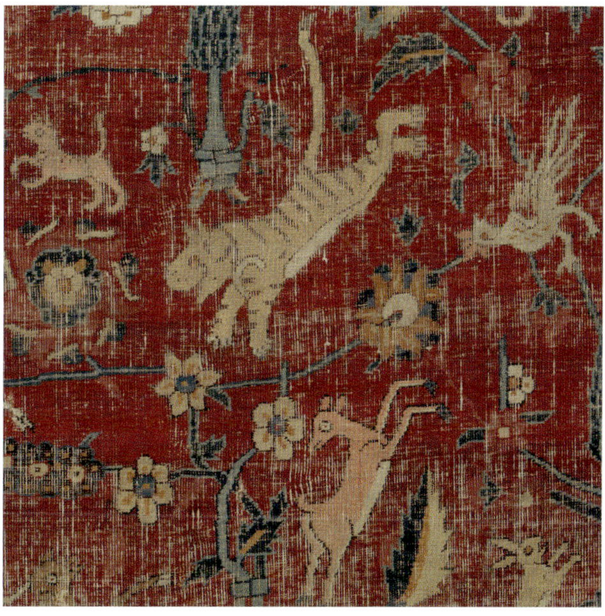

A tiger and other animals dart across the field in different directions.

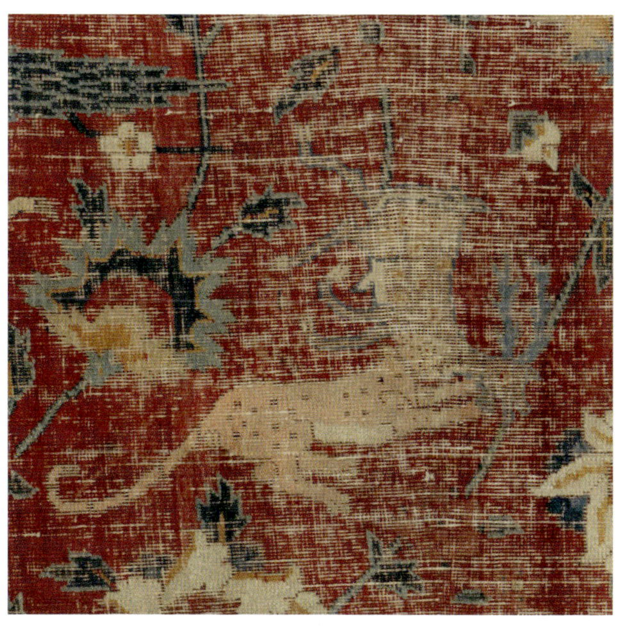

A hunting cheetah captures a deer.

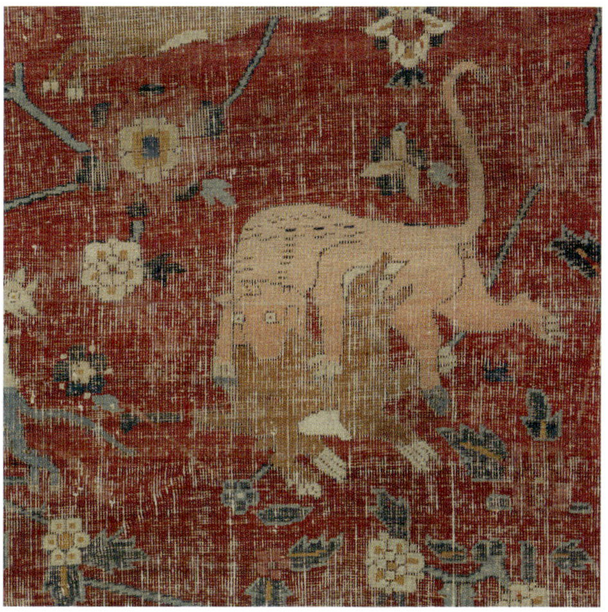

A pale-coloured Asiatic male lion pounces upon a brown sloth bear – a bear with markedly long claws.

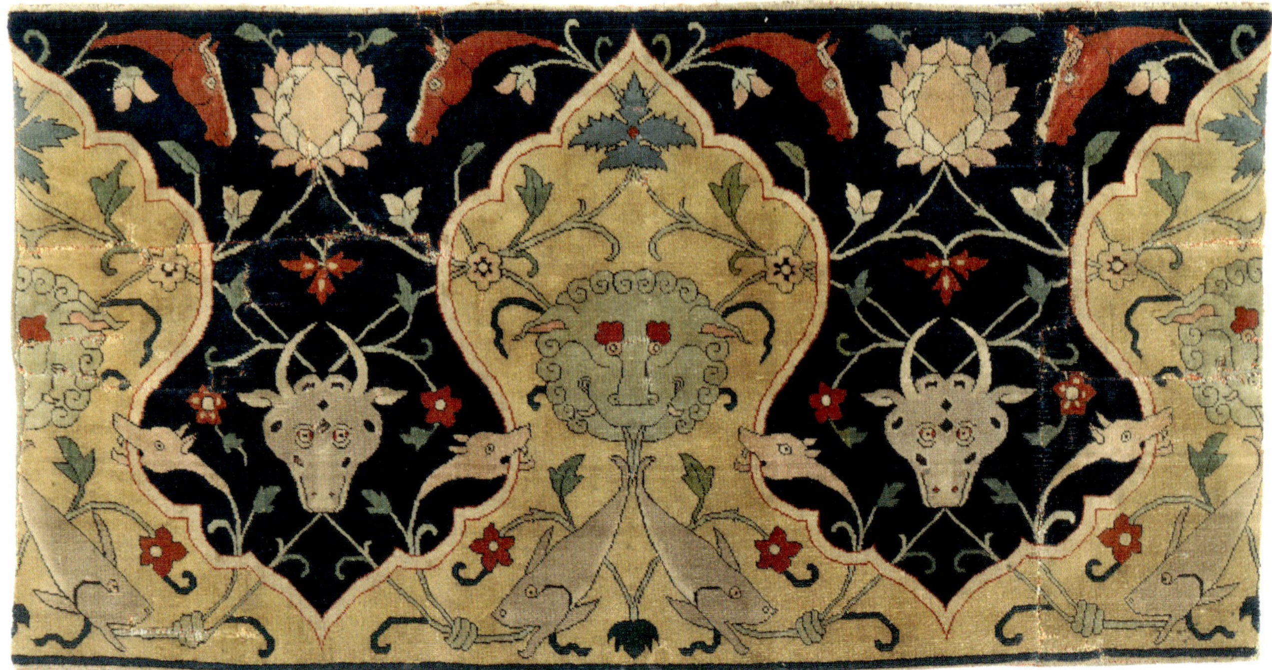

Carpet fragment with grotesque-animal design,

Safavid period, late 1500s–early 1600s
Made in Herat, Khurasan region (today in Afghanistan)
Silk warps and wefts; wool pile
78.8 x 40.7 cm
9.23

This fragment is from the side border of a carpet. It shows interlocked lobed cartouches, in yellow and dark blue. Intertwined with them is a vine scroll that bears, along with its tendrils, leaves, flowers and buds, the heads of wild animals – lions, bulls, horses, foxes and fish. The weaver has made good use of a variety of shades for some of the colours to highlight the features of the animals, particularly the horses' faces, the fishes' bellies and the bulls' noses and ears.

Seven other fragments from the original carpet survive in collections around the world, four of which are from the main field, which has a dark-blue ground filled with swirling vines bearing the heads of other animals, including elephants, rams, antelopes, cockerels and other birds. The prototype for the carpet's design is found in the miniature paintings of the Timurid style produced in Iran and Afghanistan in the fourteenth and fifteenth centuries, which in turn borrowed elements from the arts of the Seljuks in northern Mesopotamia, the Levant and Egypt of the twelfth and thirteenth centuries.

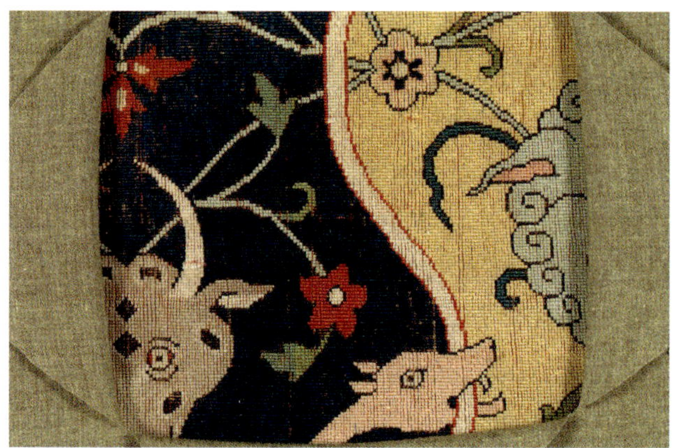

The count of the fine knotting of the pile of this carpet is approximately 500 knots per square inch, or about 78 knots per square centimetre. The knots are measured and counted on the back of the carpet. The back can be seen here, through an opening in the lining.

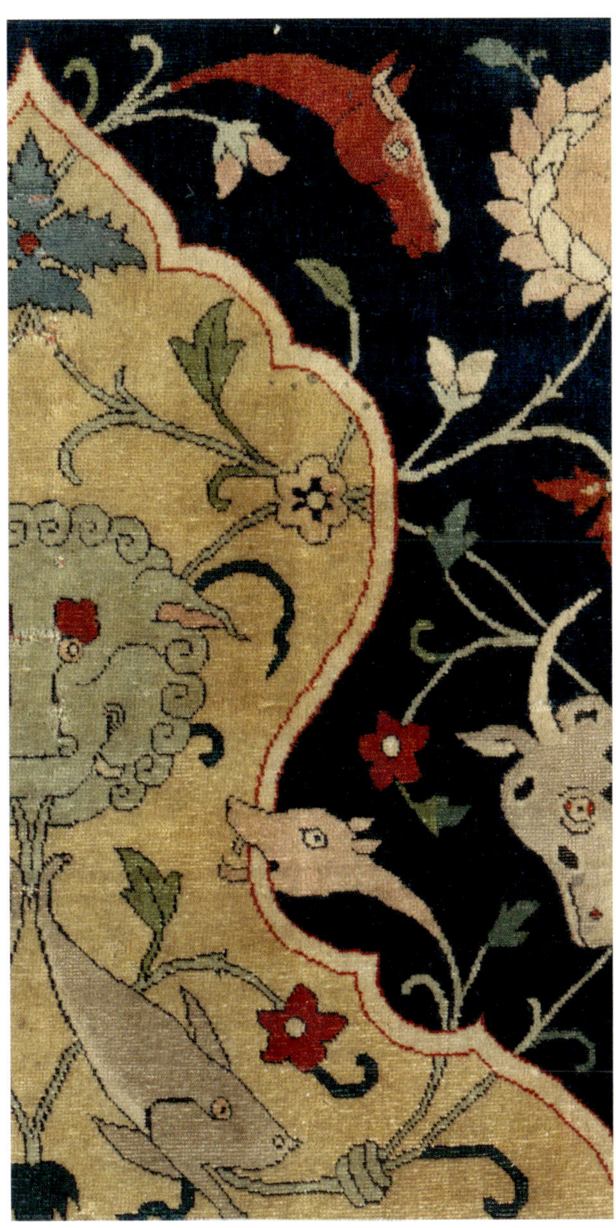

The delicate vine scrolls meander effortlessly between the yellow-ground cartouche and the dark-blue one.

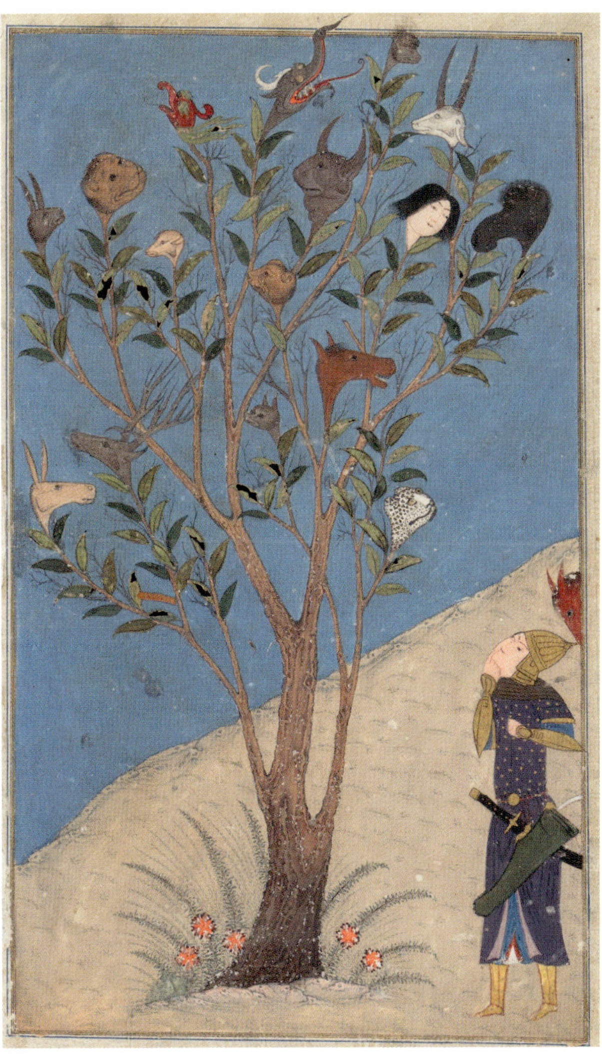

This Timurid-style miniature painting is an example of the kind of illustrations that inspired the design on carpet fragment 9.23. *Eskandar Contemplates the Talking Tree*, a miniature painting of Eskandar (the Persian name for Alexander the Great) in *The Shahnameh (The Book of Kings)* by Ferdowsi (about 940–1020), painted in Shiraz, Iran, about 1430. The Bodleian Libraries, University of Oxford, MS Ouseley Add. 176, fol. 311v.

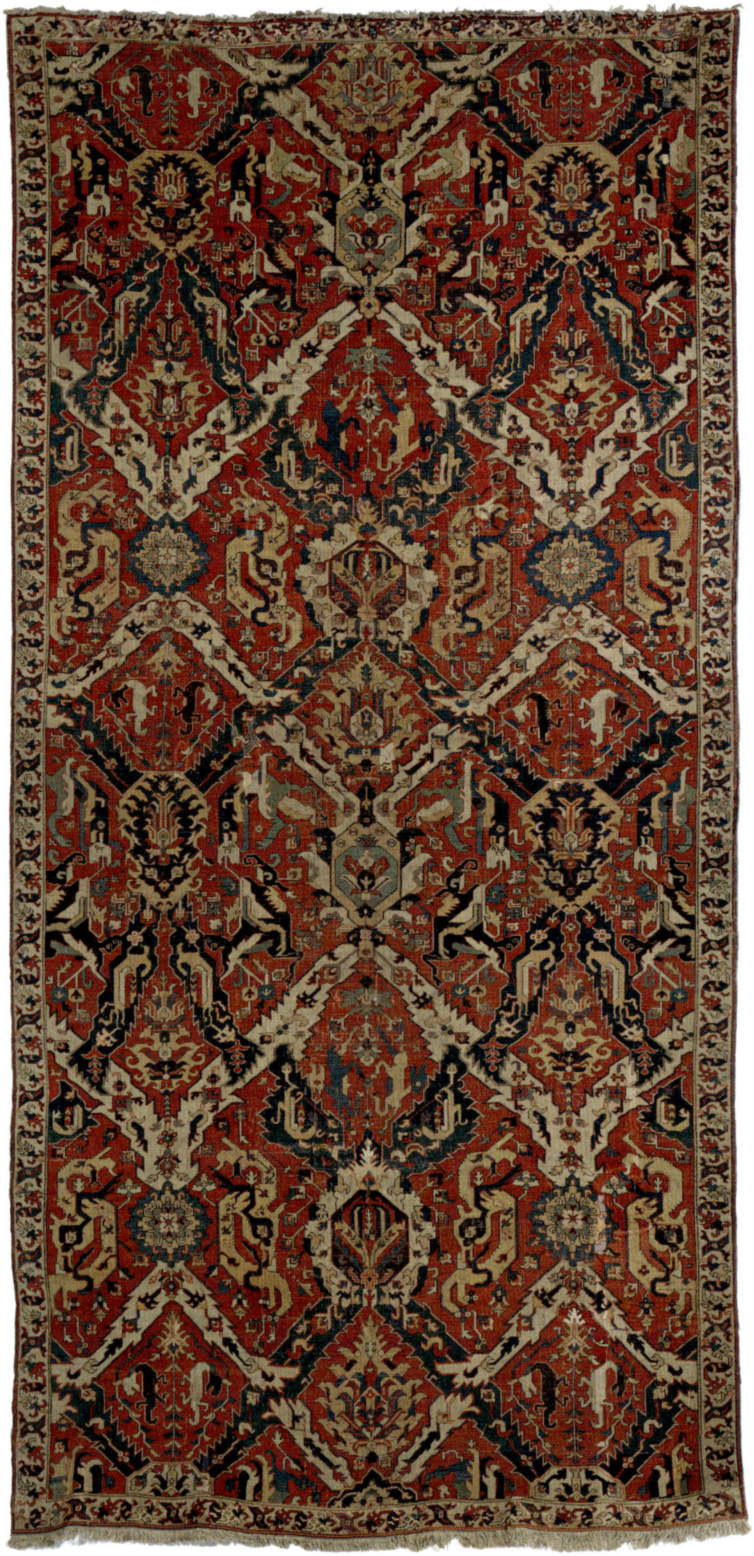

Dragon carpet,

Safavid period, about 1600–1700
Made in Shemakha, Shirvan, Azerbaijan
Wool warp and weft; wool pile
505.5 x 243.9 cm
9.38

Two vegetal lattices, one white and one blue,
criss-cross each other to form a trellis with
diamond-shaped voids or compartments.
In each of these voids is placed a single
animal or a pair of animals, some real and
some mythological. The eight yellow 'S'-
shaped creatures – four in each of the two
rows where they appear – are the dragons
after which this type of carpet is named.
The other rows of voids hold pairs of fawns

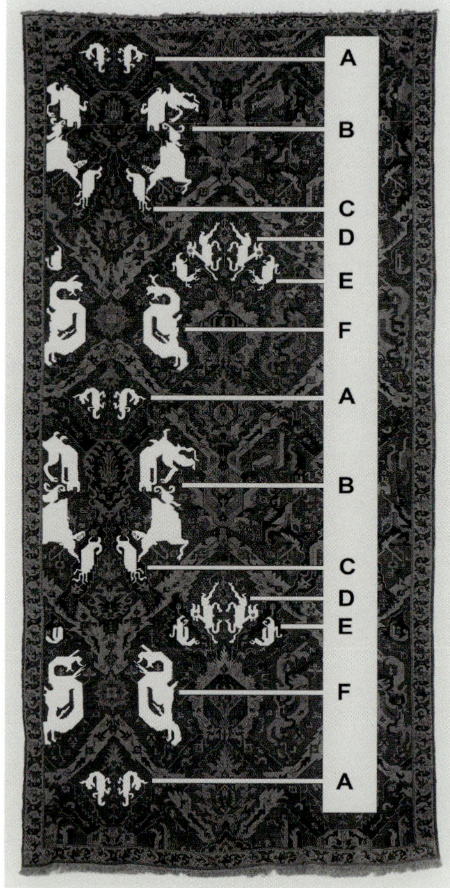

looking over their backs and away from each other, and pairs of lions and wild asses locked in combat. Amongst the vegetal decoration on the broader parts of the blue lattice are placed ducks and pheasants. These birds are the hardest to spot in this highly abstracted floral and figural composition.

This carpet is an example of a genre produced in the Caucasus region. These carpets were commercial products and sought after for their bold design and colour schemes. The motifs of the dragons, the lions and wild asses originated in China, on textiles and ceramics brought to the Middle East. They were adopted in Iran and used in an adapted form on Persian carpets, which in turn became the prototype for these designs.

Left: The modified image of carpet 9.38 shows, in white silhouette, the shapes and locations of the pairs of animals and birds that appear on the left half of thecarpet, which is a mirror image of its right half, plus the pairs of animals (D and E) which span the middle of the carpet.

A. Fawns.
B. Lions and wild asses in combat.
C. Pheasants.
D. Goat-like quadrupeds.
E. Ducks.
F. Dragons.

Dragon carpet,
Safavid period, about 1700
Made in Shemakha, Shirvan, Azerbaijan
Wool warps and wefts; wool pile
454.7 x 190.5 cm
9.42

On this dragon-carpet the design has degenerated into a very abstract form, where not only the animals cease to exist, but also the palmettes lose their distinctiveness. This type of debasement of pattern is usually a result of a weaver repeatedly copying a design without understanding its meaning.

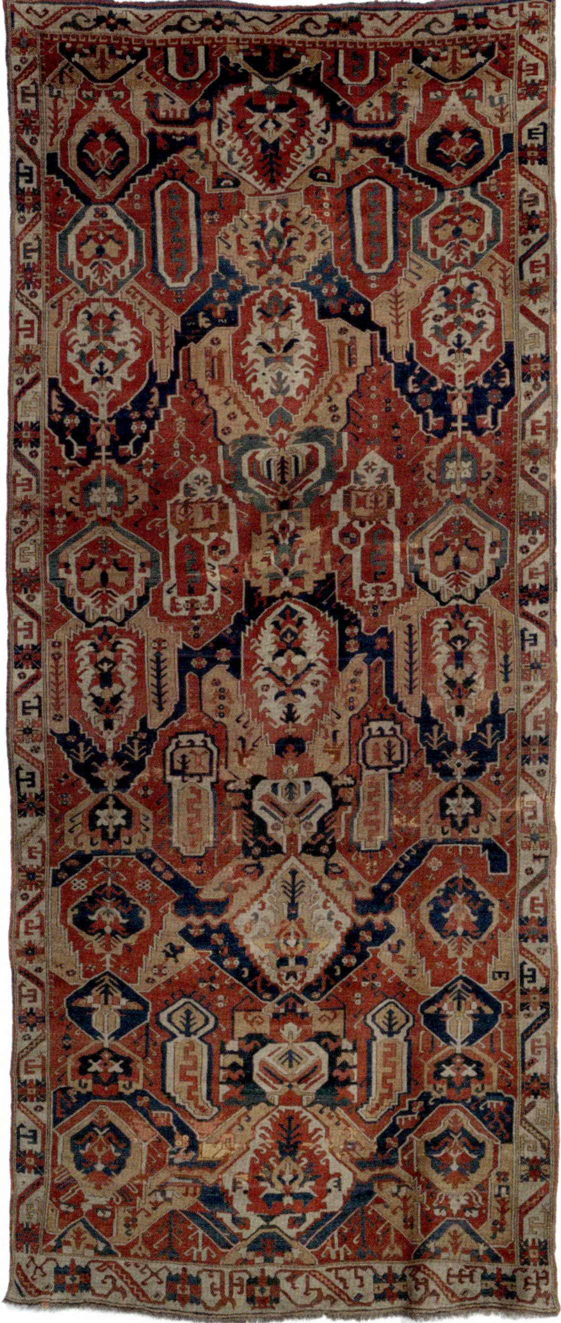

Burrell purchased this carpet in 1932 from Christie's, the London-based auction house, for £283 – more than he subsequently paid for the dragon carpet opposite (carpet 9.38), which he acquired from the dealers Balian & Son in 1939 for only £225, a bargain price given its greater artistic quality.

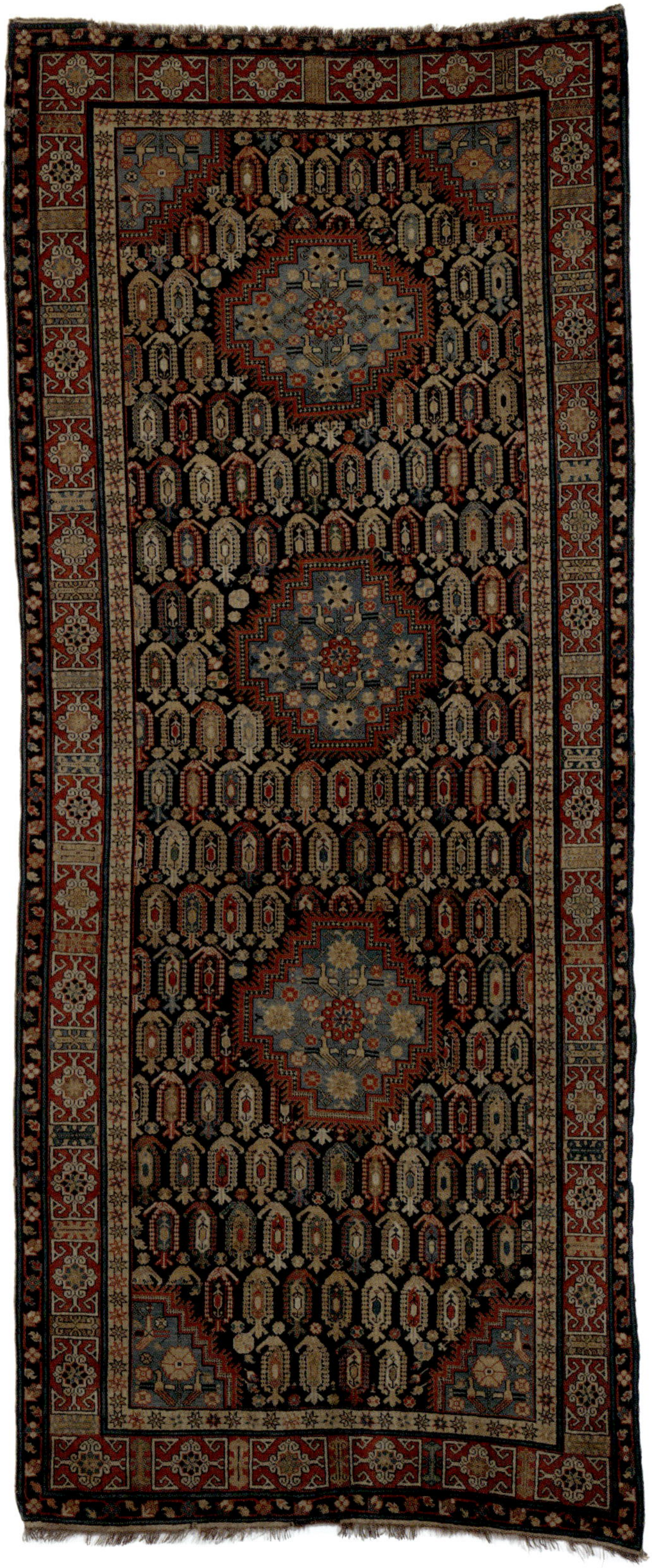

Carpet with *boteh* motif,
about 1800
Made in Khila, Baku district, Azerbaijan
Wool warps and wefts; wool pile
370.8 x 157.5 cm
9.82

In each of the three blue medallions on this carpet
two pairs of birds spread their wings and soar
amongst rosettes and small flowers. In marked
contrast, the field surrounding these medallions is
occupied by offset rows of multicoloured *boteh*
motifs. The birds are depicted in a geometric
abstract style, with straight, thick lines for their
wings and diagonal thin ones for their tails. In an
attempt to visualize perspective, the birds' inner
wings are illustrated smaller in size than their
outer ones, giving the impression that they are
flying upwards and away from each other.

Carpet with animal motifs,

about 1800–1900
Made in Western Iran
Wool warps and wefts; wool pile
279.4 x 106.7 cm
9.99

The ten vertical bands that fill the field of this carpet are crossed by horizontal rows of small geometrical motifs arranged in a directional repeat pattern. The bottom and top rows of the repeat pattern are occupied by quadrupeds of two types. One set resemble horses with their ears spread apart, one to the front and one to the back. The other set have gazelle horns. In between these two rows are rows of other motifs, including water vessels, pendant-like charms, *botehs* and floral elements. Many types of Persian, Caucasian and Kurdish tribal carpets bear animal motifs that are simply shaped and subtly inserted into the field or the border.

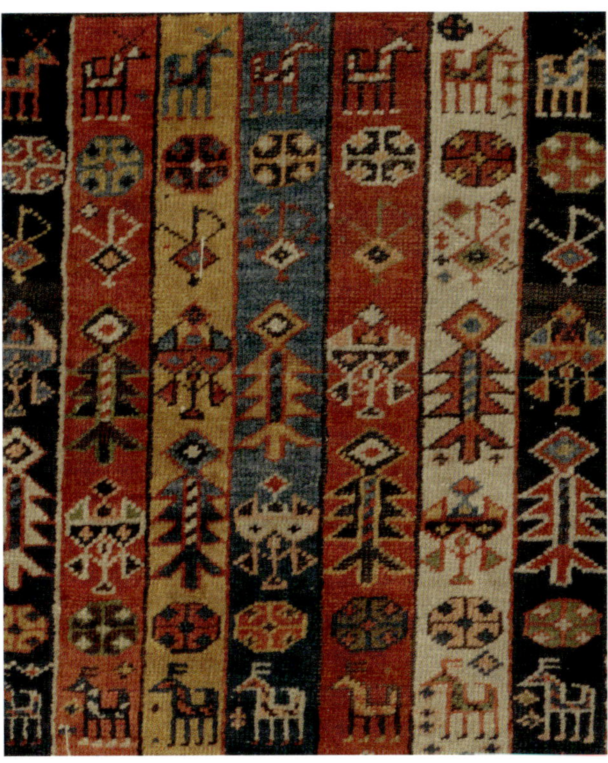

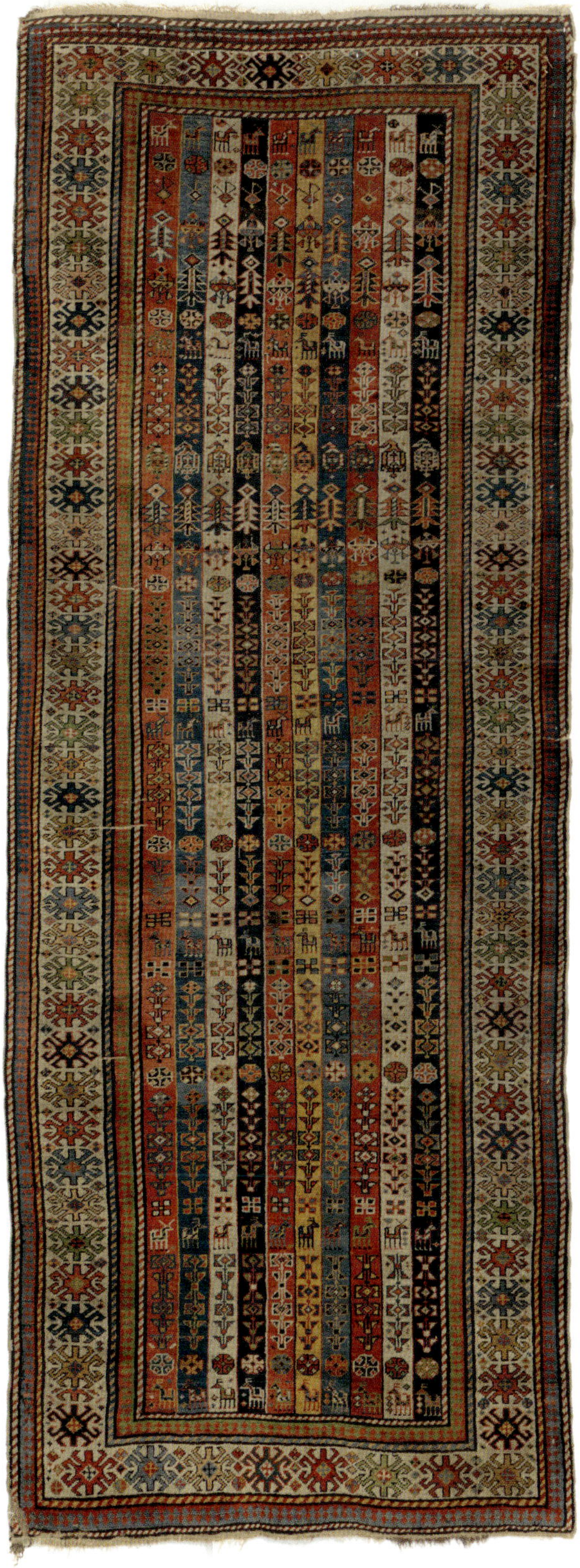

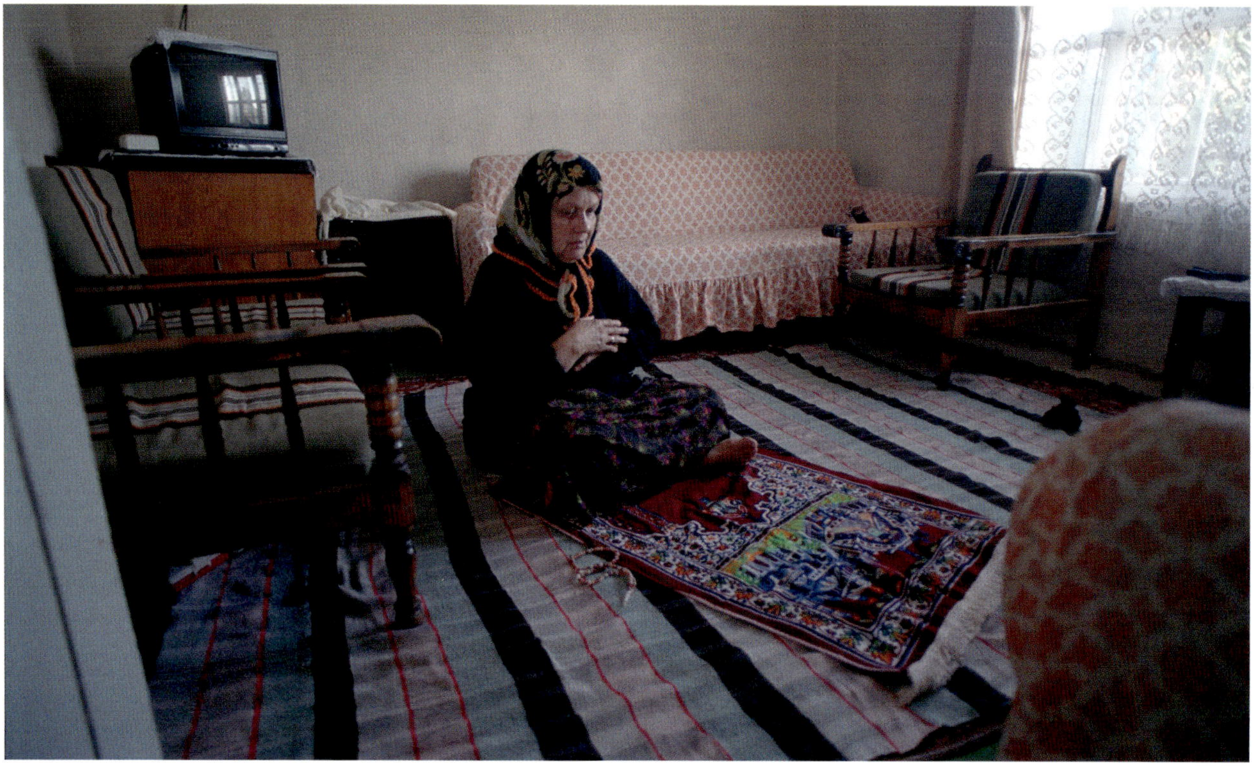

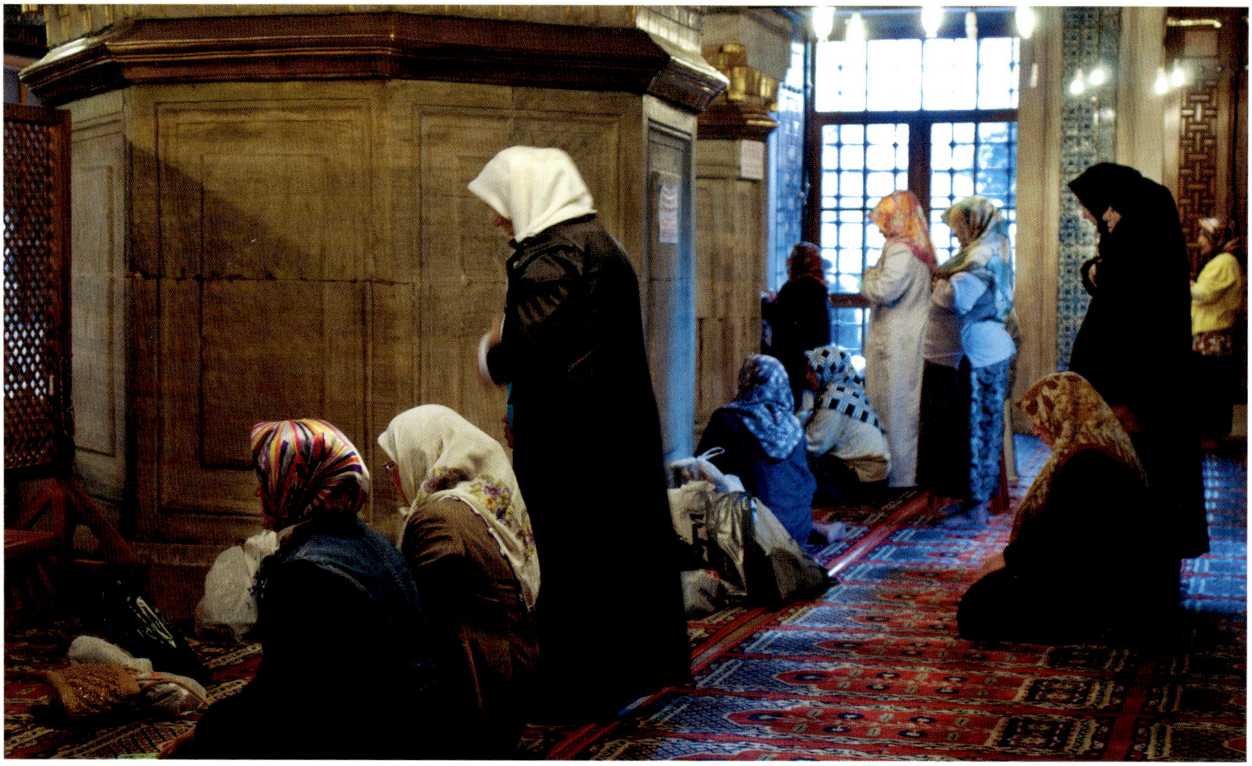

Carpets made for Prayers

Prayer rugs are a type of floor covering designed to be used when performing the five daily prayers of the Islamic faith. They can be made of a variety of materials, from animal skins and felt mats to printed and embroidered textiles, flat-woven rugs and knotted-pile carpets. Their purpose is to provide a clean surface to pray on, and once the prayers are completed they are rolled up or folded away until they are next needed. In themselves, prayer rugs are not sacred objects, but they are prized as symbols of piety.

Burrell confined himself to collecting prayer rugs of knotted-pile carpet, and the collection holds 27 of this type. Of these, 23 come from the Anatolian villages of Ladik, Ghiordes (today Gördes), Kula and Kirsehir in Turkey, and the remainder are from the region of Shirvan in Azerbaijan and from Senneh (today Sanandaj) in the Kurdish region of Iran. Archival photographs of Hutton Castle show some of these prayer rugs spread on the floors of various rooms, by beds and by fireplaces, and the smallest ones laid on large tables in the drawing room and the hall. Burrell also lent a number of them to museums around Britain.

The most common characteristics that differentiate prayer rugs from other floor coverings are their proportions and size, usually associated with the floor space a single worshiper needs to kneel and prostrate on, touching the ground with the forehead when praying. A further distinguishing feature of a prayer rug is its directional layout, with a clear distinction between the top and bottom parts of the rug. This commonly includes the presence of a niche- or arch-composition in the field of the rug, representing the architectural prayer niches and arches found in the prayer halls of mosques. This design is both symbolic and practical – indicating the end of the rug which the forehead should touch when praying.

The Burrell Collection's prayer rugs were made for individual domestic worship. The 23 Anatolian ones were woven by village women in farming communities, who sourced their materials and dyes locally and wove their rugs on looms set up at home. The sale of these rugs helped supplement the women's incomes. Their designs would have been learnt by heart and passed on from mother to daughter, with the prototypes being much earlier prayer rugs made in towns for the Ottoman court and the urban elite.

Opposite, above: A Muslim woman sits in prayer on a prayer rug in her home in the town of Mulga in south-west Turkey. She has laid out her rug in a direction that enables her to face Mecca; her prayer beads are laid by her side.

Opposite, lower: In the women's section of the Blue Mosque in Istanbul, lengths of modern machine-made carpets are laid on the floor in rows. These carpets are decorated with designs representing the arch and niche compositions found on traditional prayer rugs, encouraging worshippers to take their places for prayer in an organized way.

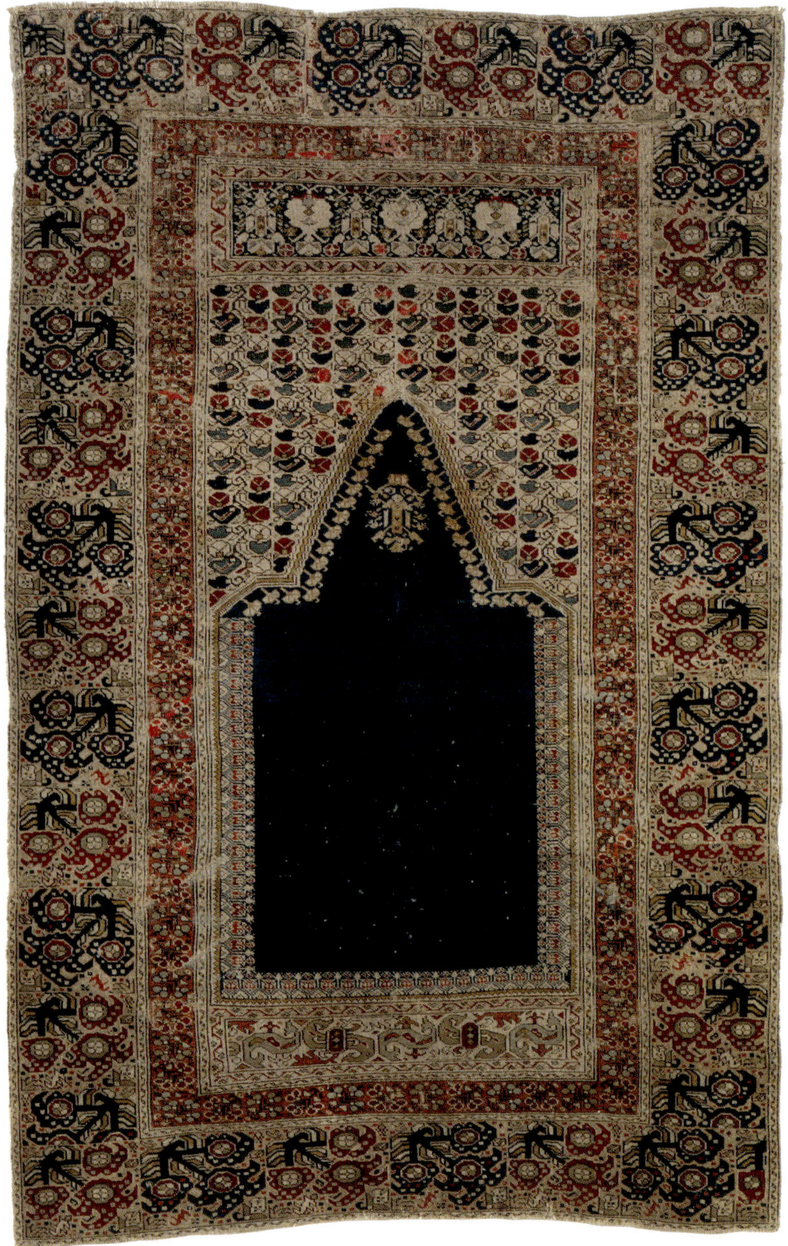

Ghiordes prayer rug,

Ottoman period, about 1800–1900
Made in Ghiordes (today Gördes), Anatolia, Turkey
Wool warps and wefts; wool pile with cotton inserts
182.9 x 119.4 cm
9.45

An oval-shaped ornament hangs under the pointed arch at the top of the dark-blue niche shown on this carpet. This ornament represents one of the glass oil lamps that were traditionally hung in Turkish mosques, which in turn are a metaphor for the illuminating divine presence of God in the world. The analogy between the niche, the lamp, the mosque and God's divine light is described in the Qur'an (*Sura*, or chapter, 24, verses 35–37).

Decorative panels, filled with floral motifs, frame the niche, and these are surrounded by a border containing floral repeat patterns. The inner edges of the niche are also decorated with floral motifs – white carnations under the arch and a band of very small, delicate red-and-white flowers on the sides and lower edge of the niche.

Ladik prayer rug,

Ottoman period, about 1802
('year 1217' in Arabic script woven
into the rug, the date by the
Islamic Hijri calendar)
Made in Ladik, Anatolia, Turkey
Wool warps and wefts; wool pile
200.7 x 111.8 cm
9.57

Two visual symbols associated with
prayer have been added to the niche
depicted on this carpet. Above the
tip of the arch is placed a recumbent
crescent moon. It resembles the
brass crescent-moon finials that
adorn the tops of minarets and
mosque domes – symbolizing the
Islamic lunar calendar, and a sign
that the building is a place of worship.

Within the red niche is placed a water
vessel – a symbol of the cleanliness
required to approach prayer. From
the base of this vessel grows a floral
shrub, which spreads to occupy
the whole niche. Some have
interpreted this as a representation
of the Tree of Life, an ancient Middle
Eastern concept of a sacred tree
associated with the source of life
and with longevity, which survived
into the Islamic period and became
associated with the heavenly tree of
knowledge and of eternal life that is
situated in Paradise.

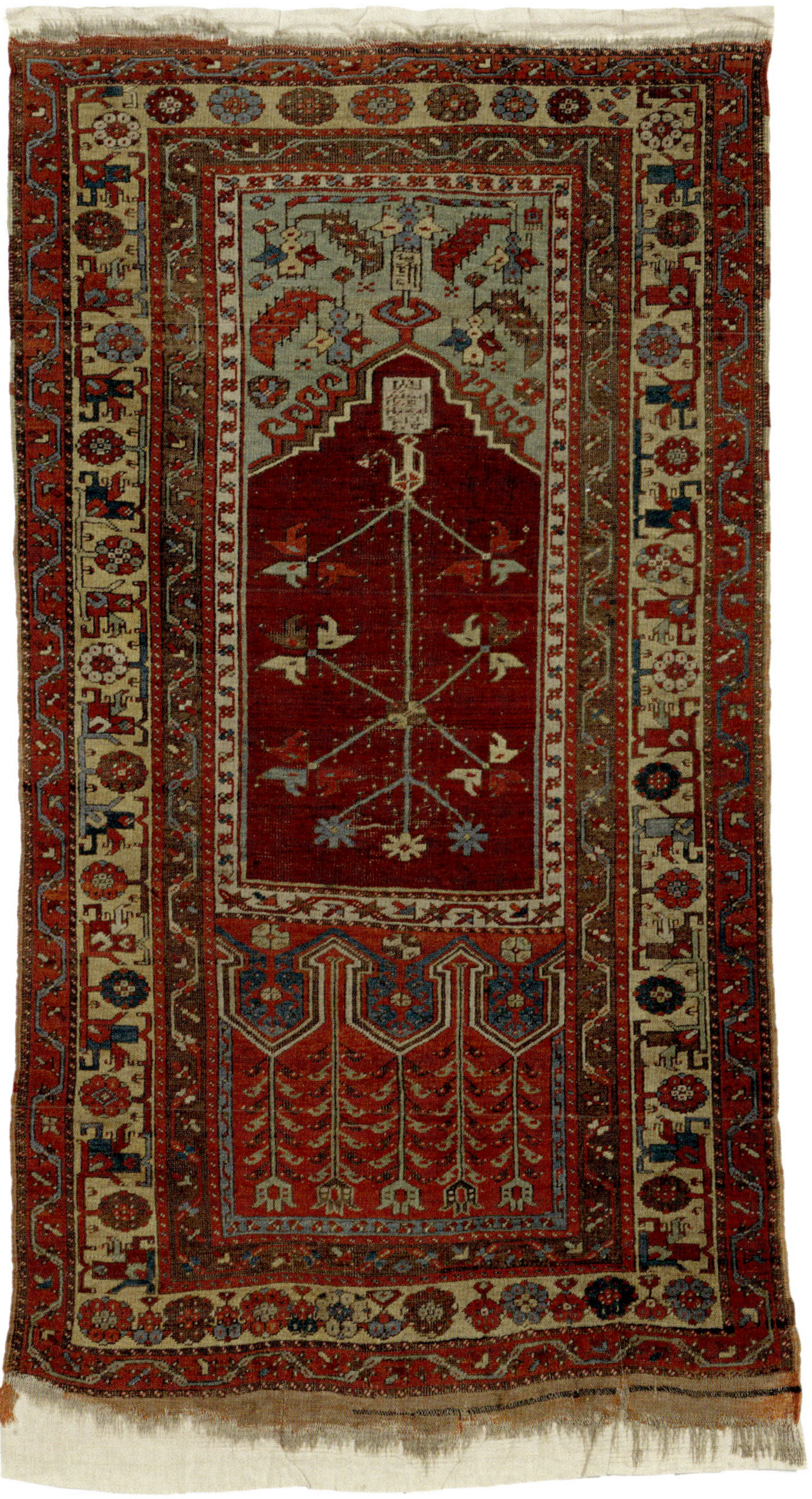

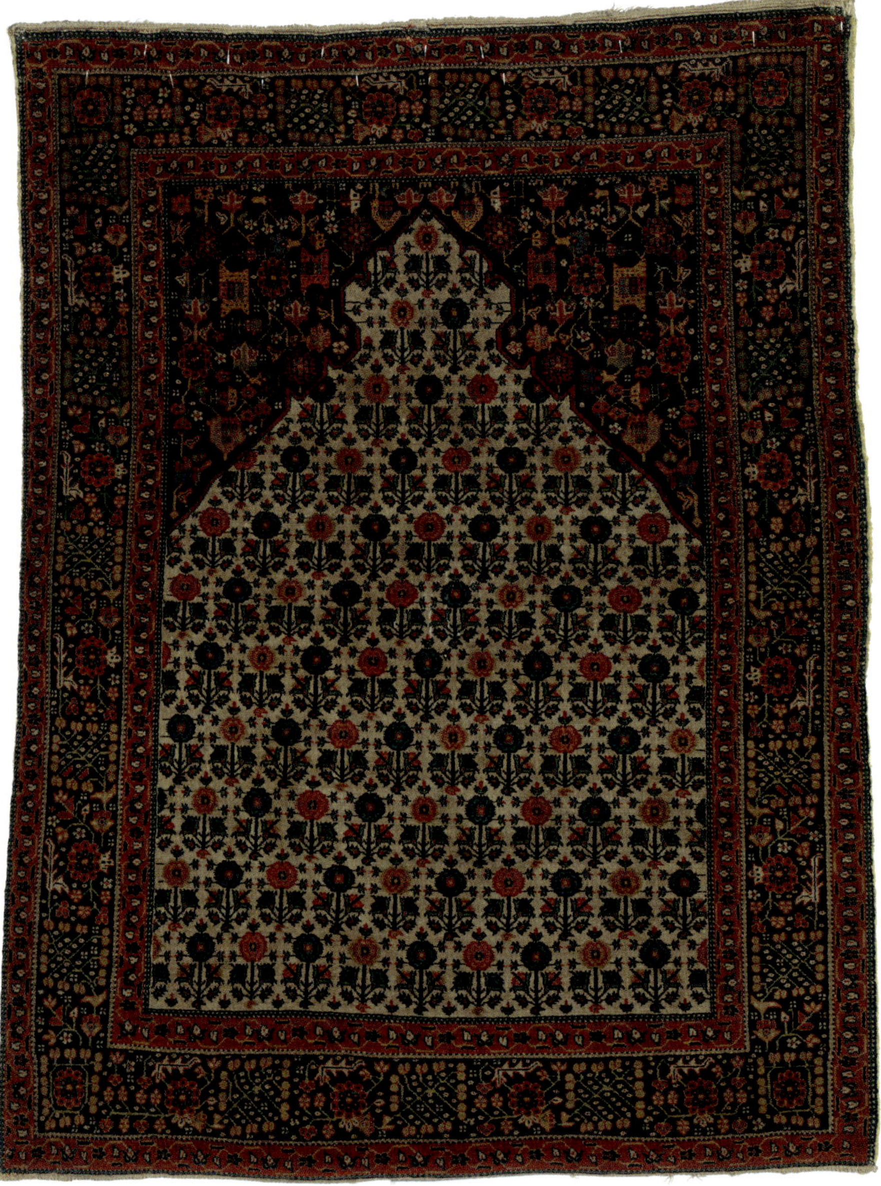

Senneh prayer rug,
Qajar period, about 1800–1900
Made in Senneh (today Sanandaj),
Kurdish region, Iran
Cotton warps and wefts; wool pile
149.9 x 111.8 cm
9.68

A repeat pattern of floral motifs fills the ivory-coloured part of the field of this carpet, with rows of blue, pink and beige flowers arranged in a staggered manner. The remarkable contrast between the lower part of the field's light colour and the darkness of both the arch above it and the surrounding border makes the rug's design resemble a window with drapes pushed aside from it, rather than a recess in a wall acting as a prayer niche.

Burrell purchased this rug in 1933 from A Balian & Son, London, and described it as being a 'Genuine Persian Senna Kurdistan Rug'. Senneh and the villages surrounding it, where this rug was made, had a thriving cottage weaving industry, dominated by female weavers and organized by the heads of the settled Kurdish tribes.

Marasali prayer rug,
Period of Russian rule, about
1838 ('year 1253' in Arabic
script woven into the rug,
the date by the Islamic Hijri
calendar)
Made in Maraza, Shirvan district,
Azerbaijan
Silk warp and weft; wool pile
with silk inserts
132.1 x 106.7 cm
9.93

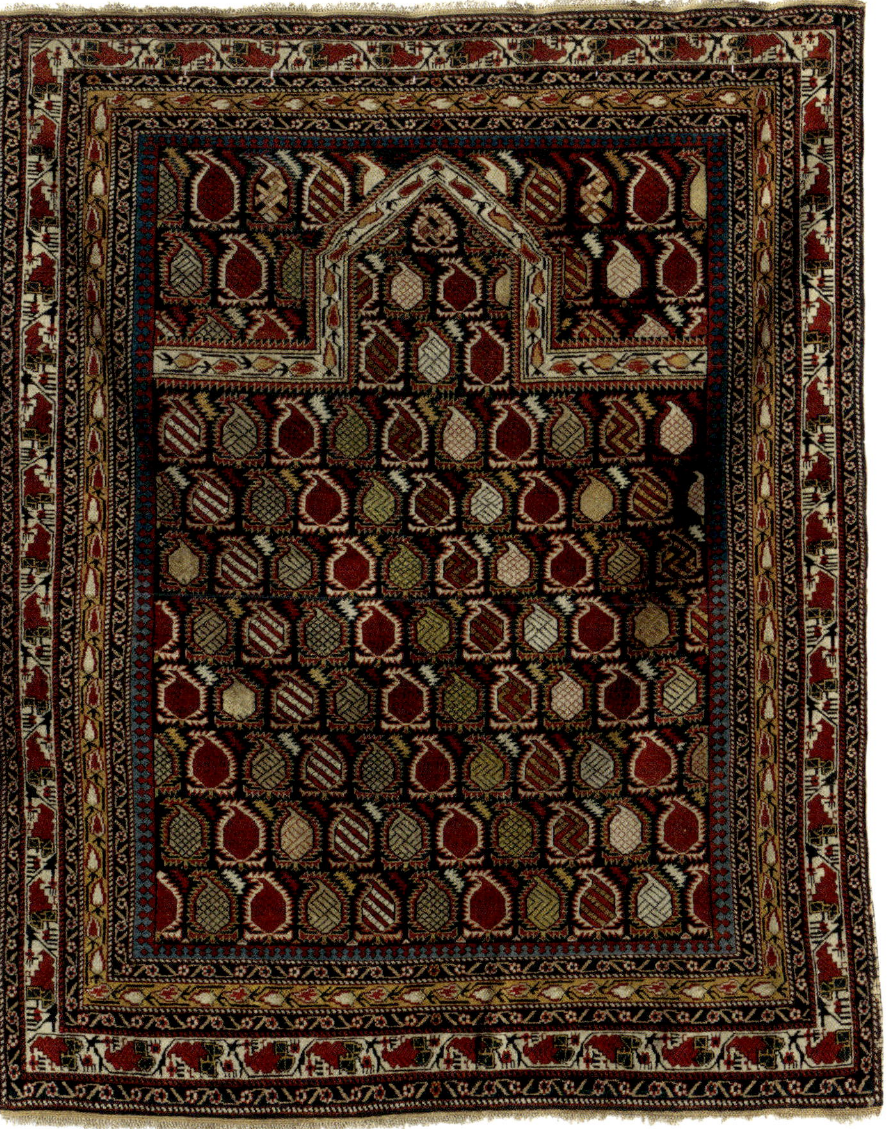

The field of this carpet is filled with coloured *boteh* motifs with serrated edges. The prayer niche is indicated by the arched band that has been superimposed on the repeat pattern within the field.

The weaver of this rug has chosen to weave the date of her work into the carpet. It is discreetly positioned on the left side of the arch's tip, in the dark-blue area between the arch and the ivory-coloured *boteh*. The inscription states 'year 1253' in Arabic script. The date, a lunar year equivalent to the time between 7 April 1837 and 25 March 1838, is according to the Islamic Hijri calendar.

Burrell purchased this rug in 1930, from the dealer OT Miller, London, for £60 and insured it for £100. Its delicate design and soft and subtle pile so impressed him that he described it as being extra fine and 'just like a handkerchief'.

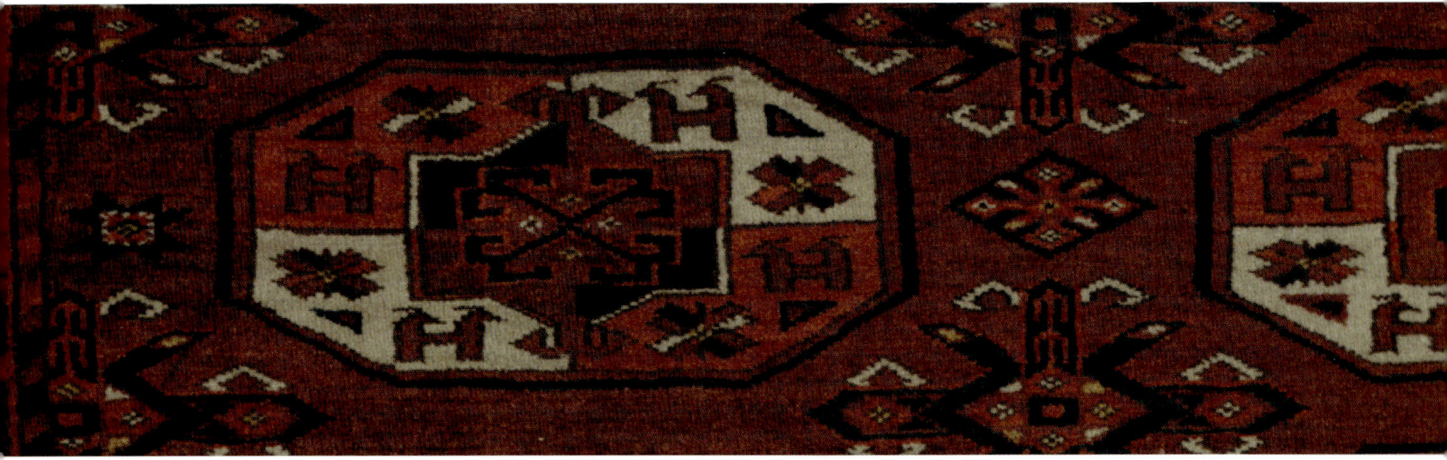

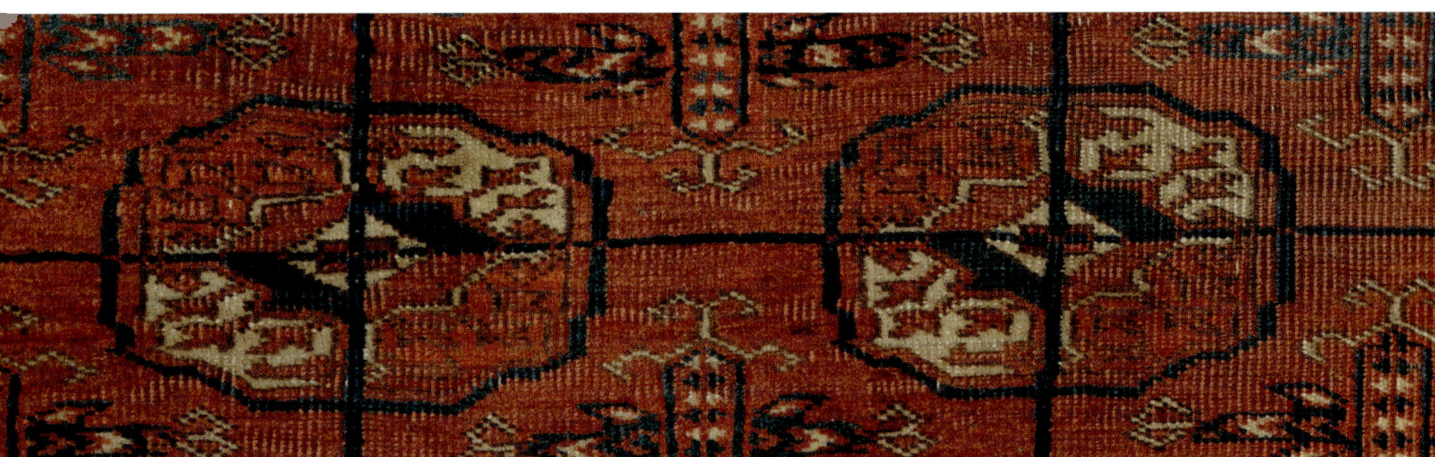

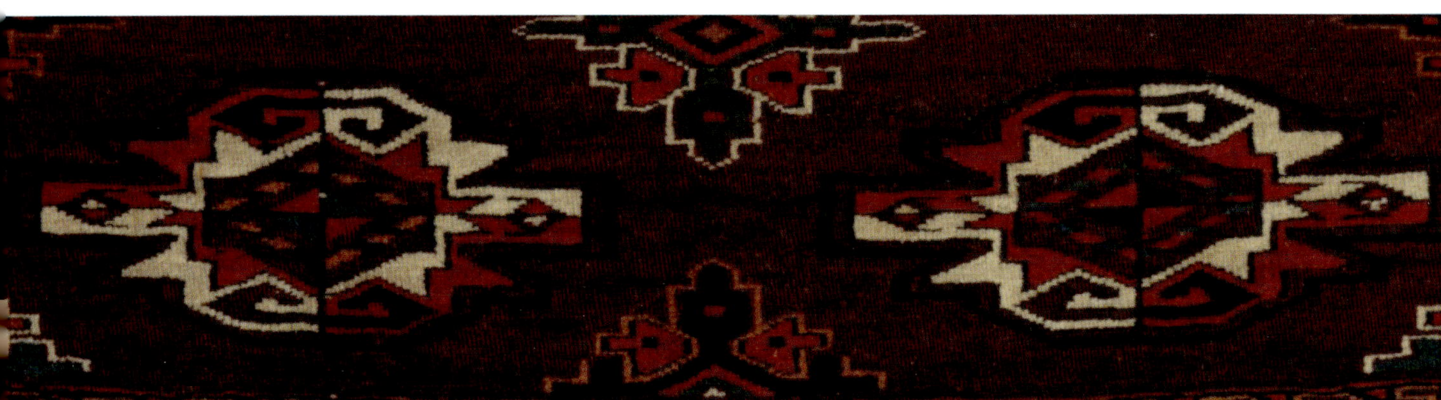

These *güls*, or tribal emblems, represent three Turkmen tribes
– the Salor, the Tekke and the Yomut. Details from carpet
fragment 9.127.f, carpet 9.107 and tent bag 9.134.

Turkmen Tribal Carpet Weaving

Although the majority of the pile carpets Sir William Burrell purchased were made in settled communities, either urban or rural, the Burrell Collection also contains a few carpets that were made by nomadic peoples, mainly the Turkmen tribes of Central Asia.

Turkmen weaving was a female affair, and mainly practised to provide the home with all the easily transportable soft furnishings it needed. This included floor coverings, drapes, a variety of storage bags and tent bands. They also wove covers for their horses, saddle bags and ornamental bands for their camels.

In addition, some of their weaving was done to create items that could be bartered for other commodities they needed, such as foodstuffs, including tea, sugar and cereals, and horses, camels, animal skins, weapons and ammunition. This bartering took place amongst the tribes and also at trading centres in the area in which they roamed. In the nineteenth century the Turkmen territories stretched from the eastern shores of the Caspian Sea and north-east Iran, across Turkmenistan, the western parts of Afghanistan and most of Uzbekistan, up to the Aral Sea. Key Central Asian cities to which they went for trade included Khiva, Bukhara and Samarkand.

In Burrell's time Turkmen carpets were misnamed after the historic Silk Road city of Bukhara (today in Uzbekistan), because this was where many of them were traded. Burrell's purchase books list a number of the so-called Bukharas being bought in 1921 and 1925. Today there are eight Turkmen items in the collection: two are storage bags and the remainder are carpets, four of which were formed of fragments and which have since been dismantled. The two complete carpets show how much use they had before entering the collection.

When looking at Turkmen weaving one is struck by the general uniformity of design and colour range, which was guided by tradition. All have a dark-red background, and all have a geometric repeat pattern. All feature several subtle shades of red in the colouring of their motifs, complemented by dark blue and white, and sometimes yellow and green colours. The motifs are mainly geometric shapes in the form of stars and octagons, which are called *güls* – flowers in Persian – even though their complex structures no longer resemble flowers. These key shapes are considered tribal emblems and through them the weaving can be attributed to specific tribes. The *güls* of several tribes are represented on Turkmen carpets in the Burrell Collection, amongst them those of the Salor, the Tekke and the Yomut.

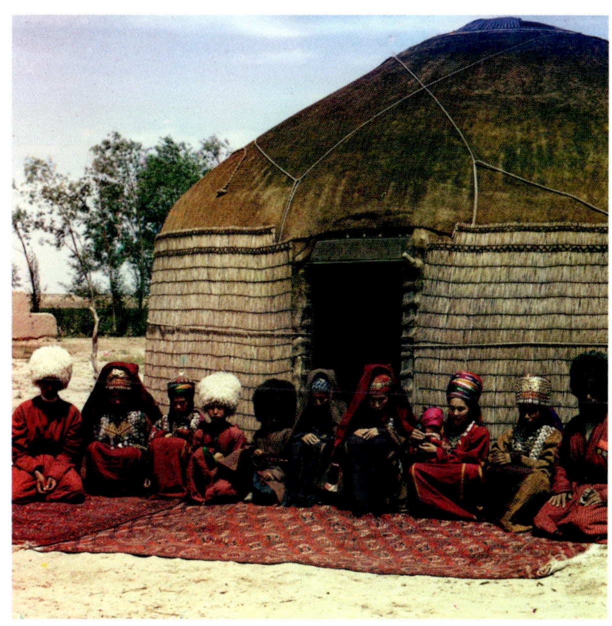

A Tekke Turkmen family sit on two of their carpets in front of their tent, Bayramaly region, Turkmenistan, early twentieth century. Library of Congress, Washington, DC, Prints and Photography Division, Prokudin-Gorskiĭ Collection, LC-DIG-prok-10086.

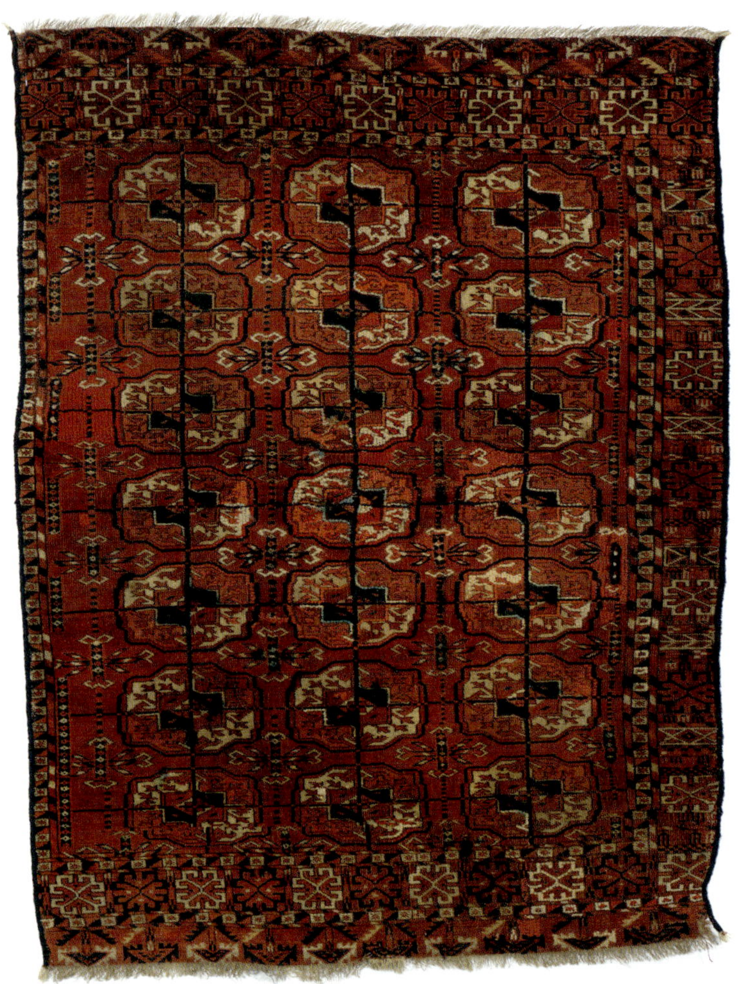

The Tekke tribal *gül* on this carpet is surrounded by other decorative motifs.

Tekke Turkmen carpet,
about 1800–1900
Made in Turkmenistan
Wool warps and wefts; wool pile
121.5 x 91 cm
9.103

This carpet shows the motif, or *gül*, emblematic of the Tekke tribe rendered in two shades of red, dark blue and white. The *güls* have been set in a grid of three vertical and seven horizontal lines. Between the *güls* there are cruciform motifs woven with the same colour combination. As is typical for Turkmen carpets woven in the nineteenth century, this carpet has a wide border at the top and bottom ends, where other motifs have been used.

This carpet has been extensively darned and some of its exposed warps and wefts have been coloured to compensate for its worn pile. When the carpet was first treated, which would have taken place before it was offered to Burrell, the shades of darning and colouring would have matched those of the pile, but, with the passage of time, the colours have aged differently, causing the once-complementary restoration to become distracting.

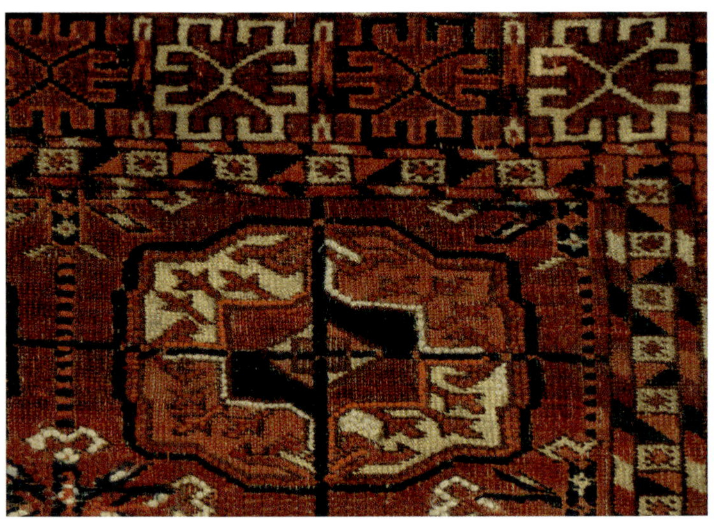

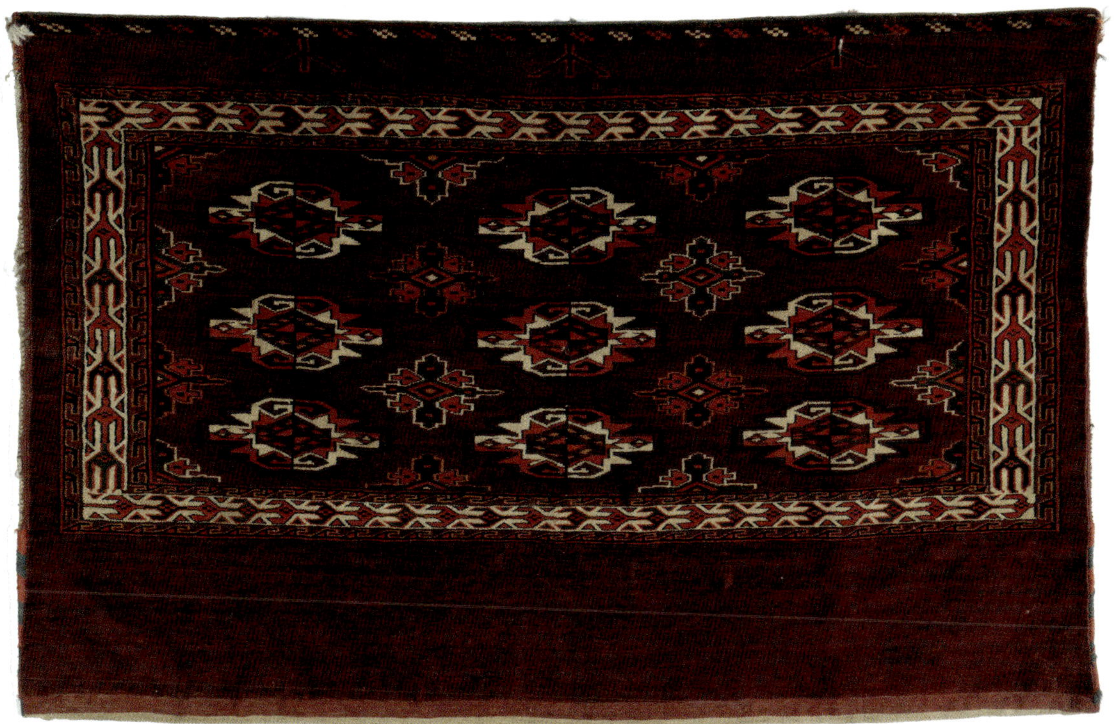

Yomut Turkmen tent bag,

about 1800–1900
Made in Turkmenistan
Wool and camel hair warps, wool weft; wool pile
76.2 x 147.3 cm
9.129

Woven in one piece, the front half of this tent bag has been knotted with pile while the back half has been woven flat and plain. The front is decorated with the Yomut tribe's *güls* – the nine geometric rosette motifs set in a grid of three by three. Interspersed between them are smaller diamond-shaped vegetal motifs.

A bag of this shape and size is called a *chuval* in the Turkmen language. It is a flat storage bag, the largest of the range of bags woven by Yomut women. Usually made in pairs and used as containers for clothes and other personal items, it would have been hung on the inside of the trellis framework of the round Turkmen tent.

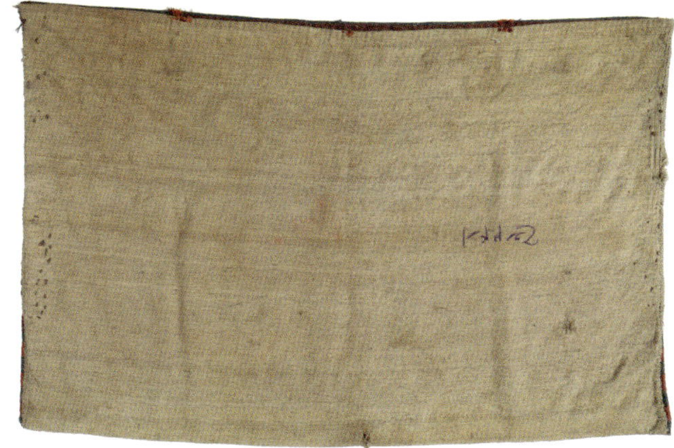

A combination of Persian numbers and letters have been hand-written in purple ink on the plain-woven back of the tent bag. They are probably the trade markings of a carpet dealer.

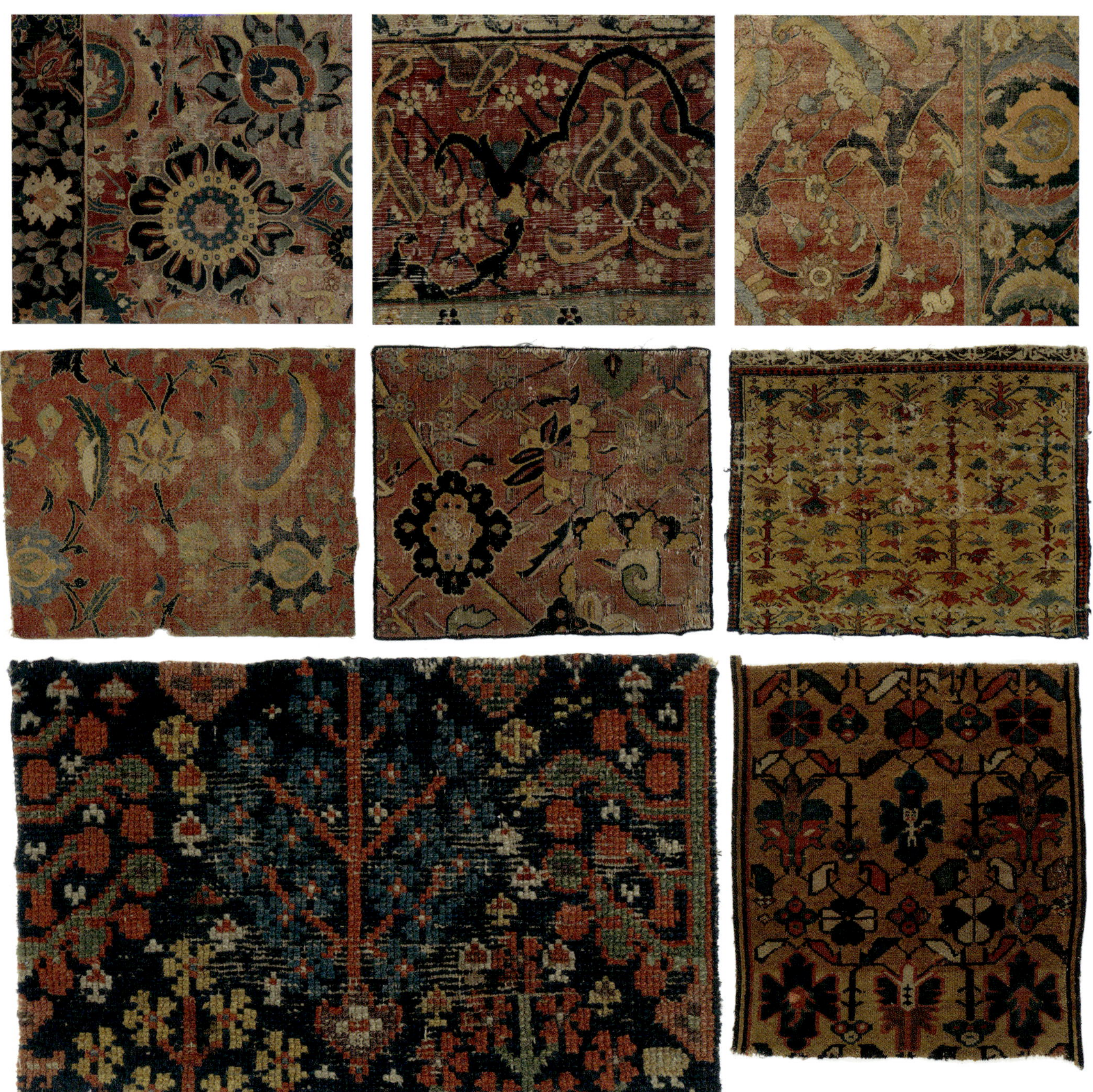

Above: These examples of historical carpet fragments in the collection show a variety of motifs and compositions, representing the richness of carpet design and the endless possibilities of pattern configuration.
Top row: details from carpet fragments 9.21.a, 9.22, 9.25.
Middle row: carpet fragments 9.36, 9.20, 9.91.
Bottom row: carpet fragments 9.79, 9.78.

Opposite: In addition to the prayer rug by the fireplace, two carpet fragments appear in this photograph of the tower sitting room at Hutton Castle from 1949. In the foreground, carpet fragment 9.77 is laid on the floor; carpet fragment 9.78 is positioned under the brass vessel on the round table. Photograph by Rupert Roddam. Glasgow Museums Archive, GMA.2013.1.1.2468.

Historical Carpet Fragments

When one surveys the carpets collected by Sir William Burrell, one cannot help but notice how many carpet fragments are amongst them. Out of the 137 objects accessioned into the pile-carpet category of the Burrell Collection, 38 are fragments. These carpet fragments are of disparate sizes. But sometimes one can be fooled by the term 'fragment', or by statements along the lines of 'it's just a third of its original size', into imagining that these items might be small. This should not be assumed, as we are reminded by the objects, especially so when standing in front of one such as carpet fragment 9.9 (pp. 10–11), which measures a little under four and a half by three and a half metres, the size of a markedly large whole carpet by today's standards.

The range of these Burrell fragments is wide, including pieces from Iran, India and Central Asia. But their ages are almost always early for their type, and this seems to be the main reason they were collected: they are rare and early survivors of an ancient craft of artistic merit.

The main causes of fragmentation include, first and foremost, wear and tear due to long use by several generations of owners. Natural materials go through natural processes of deterioration. Manufacturing methods, treatments and use accelerate these processes. Repeated washing, pest infestation, excessive fluctuations in environmental conditions and misuse are all causes for degradation.

The European interest in collecting historical and early examples of carpets led to the active seeking out of such pieces by dealers and their agents who roamed and scoured the ancient cities of the Middle East, the Indian subcontinent and Central Asia, particularly their old quarters and public buildings, such as mosques, shrines and religious schools, searching for antique carpets which, because of their age and condition, had been relegated to less important spaces within these establishments or that were no longer in use, and so were available for sale.

This led to the acquisition of dilapidated and damaged carpets. Depending on the scale and location of the damage, dealers repaired or modified the shapes of these carpets, including by cutting them up into pieces to salvage the less damaged parts and selling the pieces individually to their clients. Several Burrell Collection carpet fragments were from carpets in advanced states of deterioration, and pieces associated with them – from the same original carpets – are in other museums in Europe and North America. The most famous example is that of the Ardabil Shrine pair of carpets, which, in reconfigured forms, are at the Victoria and Albert Museum, London, and at the Los Angeles County Museum of Art. A small surplus fragment, left over from when the pair were restored, is in the Burrell Collection (carpet fragment 9.120, p. 74).

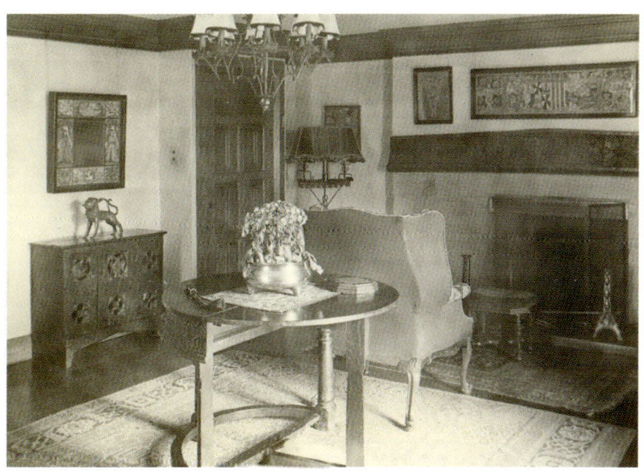

Objects in Focus

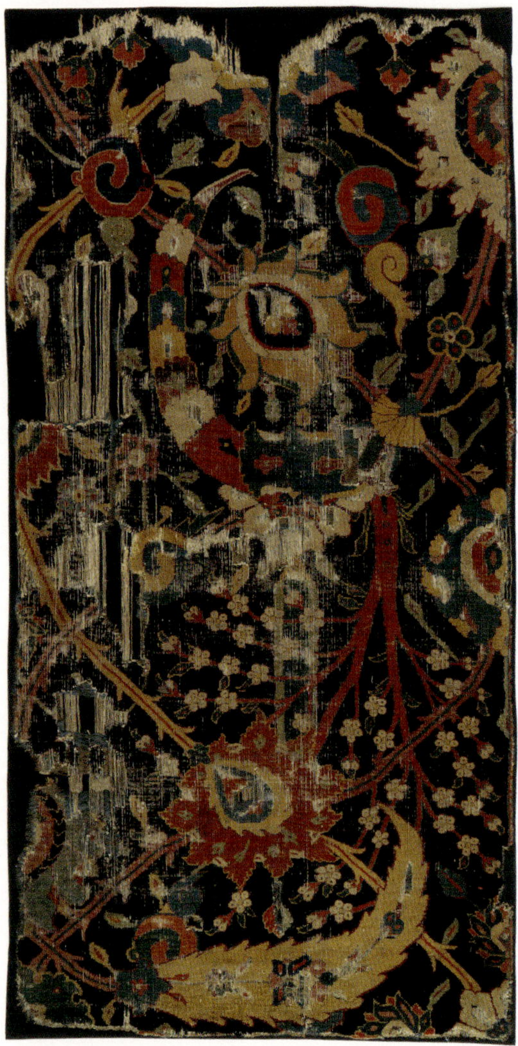

Field fragment,
Safavid period, about 1600–1700
Made in Isfahan or Kirman, Iran
Cotton warps, wool and silk wefts; wool pile
132.1 x 66.1 cm
9.15

This fragment is one of nine known to have survived
from what is considered to have been a carpet of
exceptionally high quality. One of the other eight
fragments is at the Victoria and Albert Museum,
London.

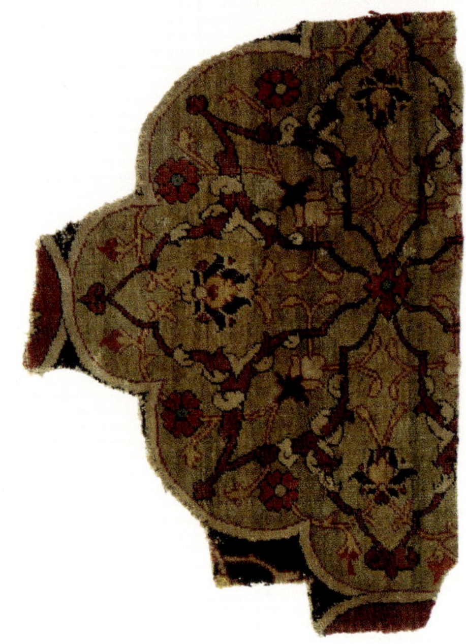

Fragment from the Ardabil Shrine carpets,
Safavid period, 1539–40 ('946' in Arabic script
woven into the rug, the date by the Islamic Hijri
calendar)
Made by Maqsud Kashani in Iran
Silk warps and wefts; wool pile
32.4 x 20.3 cm
9.120

This is a fragment from the border of one of the
pair of Ardabil Shrine carpets, reputed to have
been woven for the shrine of the Sufi mystic Shaikh
Safi al-Din Ardabili (1253–1334). By the 1880s the
Ardabil pair were significantly worn and damaged,
and were sold to Ziegler and Co., a Manchester-
based firm with offices in Iran, specializing in the
production and distribution of Persian carpets.
After repairing them, Ziegler and Co. sold the Ardabil
carpets in 1892 to the London-based carpet
dealers Vincent Robinson and Co., who restored
them using parts of one of the pair to complete the
other, resulting in one carpet at full size and one
at a reduced size. Twenty or so leftover fragments
from this restoration process were sold separately,
including this one which was later, in early 1954,
presented to Burrell by a private owner in London.

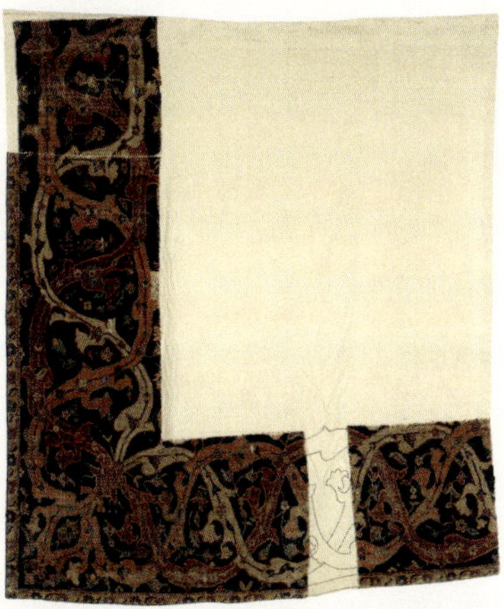

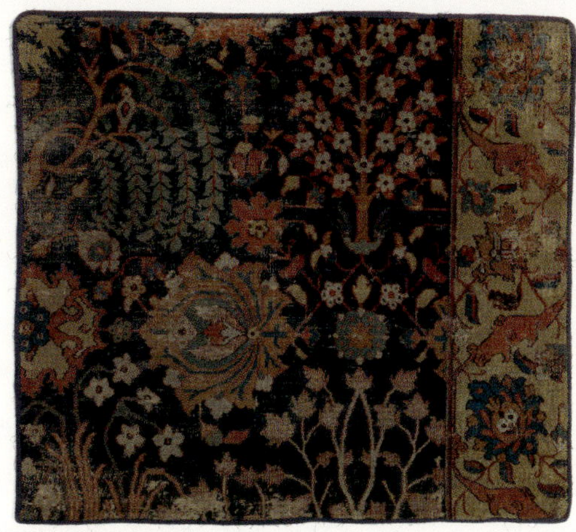

Border fragment,
Safavid period, about 1600–1700
Made in Isfahan or Kirman, Iran
Cotton warps and wefts; wool pile
137.1 x 91.4 cm
9.14

This is a border fragment from the lower-left corner of an arabesque carpet. Other fragments of this same carpet are in several museum collections, including the Museum of Fine Arts, Boston, the Louvre, Paris, and the Hermitage, St Petersburg. When Burrell purchased this fragment, its three parts had been sewn together to form a rectangle. It was subsequently dismantled to work out where its parts would have been positioned within the original carpet, as shown above.

Carpet fragment,
Safavid period, about 1600–1700
Made in Isfahan, Iran
Cotton warps, cotton, wool and silk wefts; wool pile
62.3 x 88.9 cm
9.17

The carpets specialist Dr May Beattie saw this carpet fragment as being exceptional. She commented that the combination of the yellow ground and the three-plane-lattice design of the field was uncommon, and that the choice of border design to frame it made the carpet to which the fragment had belonged even more rare and unusual.

Carpet fragment,
about 1700–1800
Made in the Kurdistan region, Iran
Cotton warps and wefts; wool pile
72.4 x 66.7 cm
9.122

A little bird can be spotted perching on the willow tree on this carpet fragment; it has become the focus of the scene because of the way the fragment was salvaged from the original carpet. The structure of this carpet drew scholarly attention, as it has many what are called in Persian *jufti* knots – pile knots that are tied round more than two warps to quicken the knotting task. This corner-cutting practice caused a weakening of the carpet's structure in the long term.

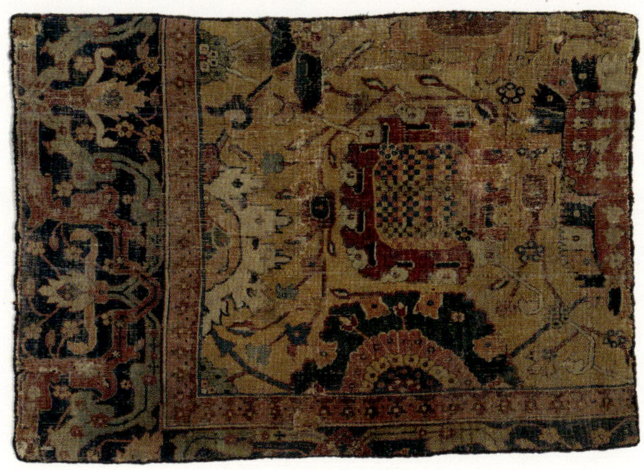

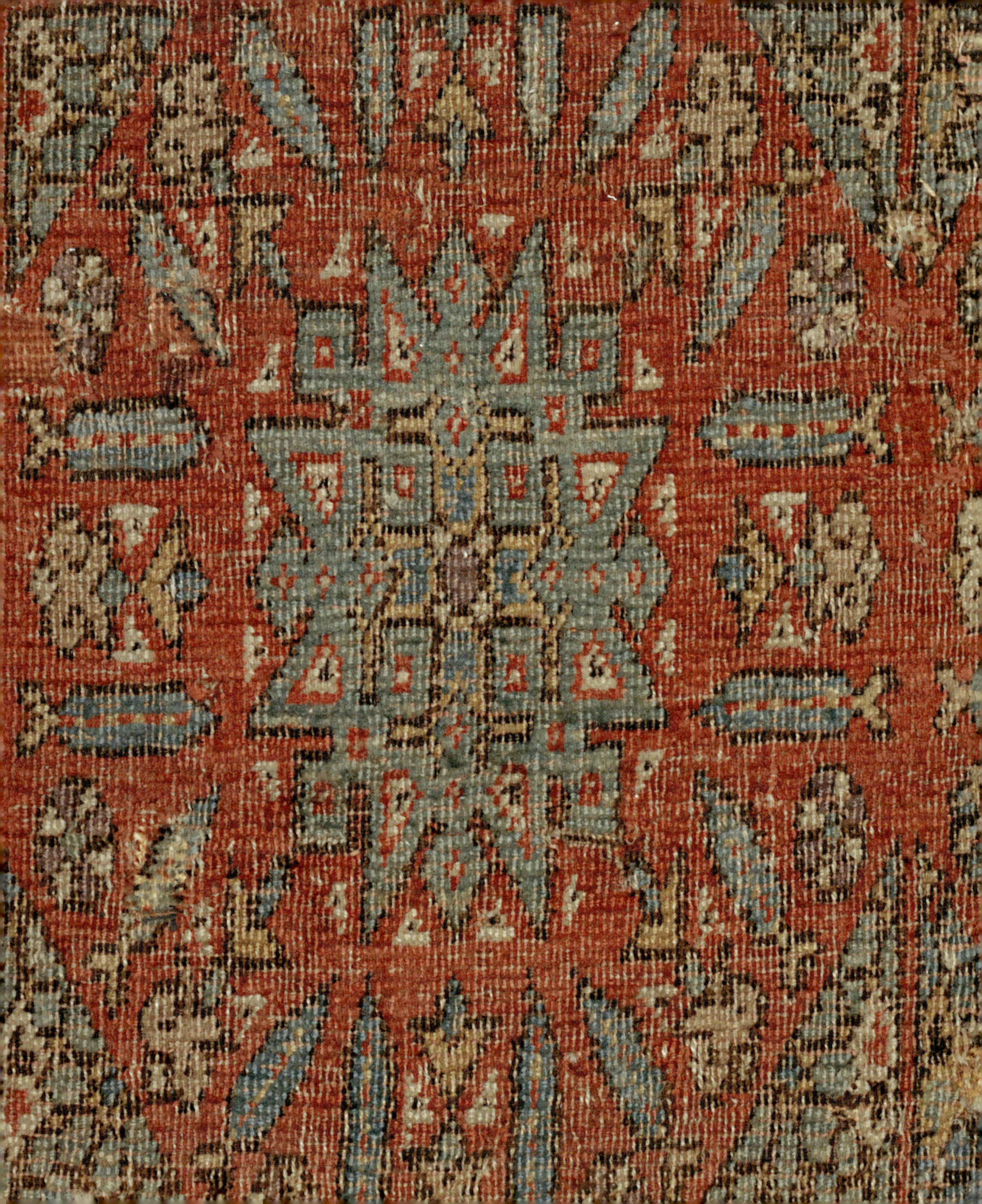

Epilogue: Influence and Transition

Sir William Burrell's belief in the value of engaging with art was aptly described by a journalist at the *Berwickshire News and General Advertiser*, who interviewed him in 1949 to mark Burrell's gift of artworks to the town of Berwick-upon-Tweed. The journalist wrote, on 10 May, that art was to Sir William's mind 'most fascinating and delightful, and at the same time a most educative hobby anyone could take up … it brushed up our geography and included our history as nothing else did, because the history and art of the country were closely interwoven'. These words tell us much about

Burrell's thoughts and attitude towards exploring and collecting artworks from across the world, including Islamic art and knotted-pile carpets. With this parting thought, a further three special carpets have been selected to conclude this journey of exploration of the Burrell Collection's Islamic carpets. Each of these carpets is a witness to the travel of ideas, the exchange of influences, and the transitions that give birth to new styles of a long-living artistic tradition – born in the Middle East and spread from Spain in the west to China in the east.

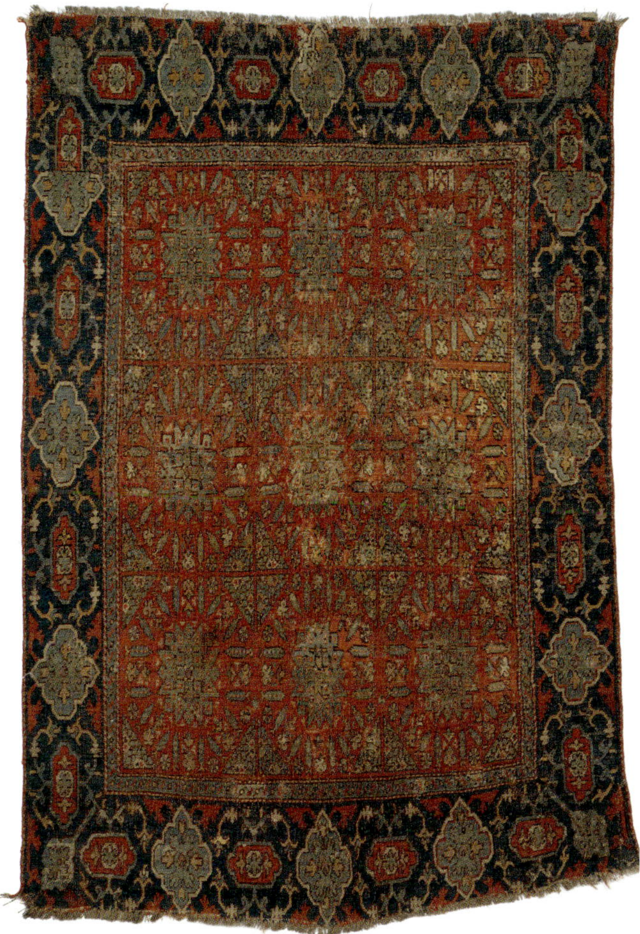

Carpet with arabesque stars,
Ottoman period, about 1500–1600
Made in Damascus, Syria
Wool warps and wefts; wool pile
154.9 x 121.9 cm
9.67

The red field of this carpet is divided into nine compartments, each holding a large, light-blue arabesque star encircled by cypress trees and framed by triangular corner pieces. The dark-blue border holds a band of alternating blue and red cartouches. Well worn, the carpet has been repaired with patches of carpet of a similar type. It is also misshapen, especially along the bottom part. This is a common occurrence in carpets that have woollen warps and wefts, caused by fluctuations in humidity and by use.

Made at the dawn of the Ottoman era, the carpet represents a short transitional phase in carpet design in the Levant – from the Mamluk period to the Ottoman – combining decorative elements from Egyptian Mamluk carpets and weaving techniques from the eastern part of the Middle East.

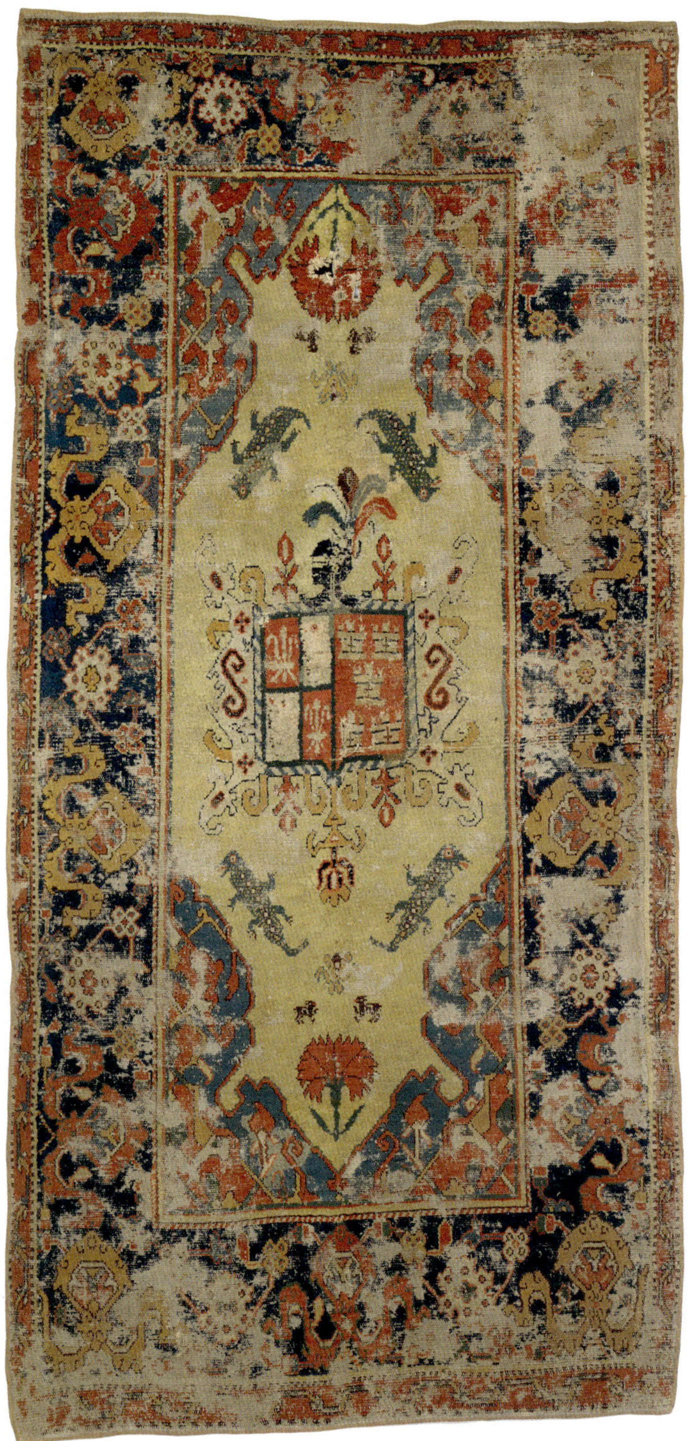

Spanish armorial carpet,

Habsburg period, about 1600–1700
Made in Cuenca, Spain
Bast warps and wefts, possibly of flax or linen;
wool pile
261.6 x 129.5 cm
9.24

The prototype design and weaving technique for this Spanish pile carpet are found in Ottoman Turkish rugs woven in Anatolia. The yellow field holds four large arabesque corner pieces. Between them are placed two red carnations illustrated in Ottoman fashion. In the centre of the field, where on the prototype there would be a medallion, there is instead a Spanish coat of arms that marks the union of two families. The sinister side (to the left from the perspective of someone carrying an armorial shield, but to the right from the perspective of the viewer), with five towers on a red ground, represents the ancestry of the woman in the union, who has been identified as being from the Heredia family. On the dexter side – the quartered side – the husband's family is represented by two fleurs-de-lis on red ground and two lions rampant on cream ground. The family denoted by this half of the coat of arms remains unknown. Four lizard-like creatures are positioned on the yellow field above and below the coat of arms. They too remain an enigma. The dark-blue border holds a vine scroll which bears white rosettes and yellow and red cloud bands.

Cuenca was one of the earliest centres for pile-carpet weaving during the Muslim presence in Spain; during the sixteenth and seventeenth centuries this weaving tradition was continued by the Mudejars and by the decedents of Muslims. They combined their cultural heritage with the tastes and needs of their Christian patrons, weaving carpets like this one.

Khotan silk carpet,
Qing period, 1800s
Made in Khotan in the historic region of East
Turkistan (today in the Xinjiang Uyghur
Autonomous Region, China)
Silk warps and weft; silk pile
226.1 x 154.9 cm
9.111

Images cannot do this carpet justice, no matter
how good they are, for they are unable to fully
convey the silkiness and subtle colourfulness
of the beautiful fine-silk pile. The light-brown
field is occupied by a geometric lattice of
delicate, light-blue stems bearing dark- and
light-blue, yellow-ochre and ivory-coloured
flowers, buds and leaves. The dark-blue border
holds a band of brown brackets formed of
long, serrated leaves with curled tips and small
flowers in pale blue, pink and beige.

The lustrous silk fibres of the pile on this carpet
have a special visual feature – the colour
shades of the border and the field appear
markedly darker or lighter depending on where
the person viewing the carpet is positioned
in relation to it. Both the properties of the silk
fibres and the directional clipping and combing
of the pile in the weaving process cause this
optical effect: as light falls on the surface it
reflects differently depending on the direction
in which the pile is lying, allowing for two sets
of colour shades to be seen.

The fringe, which is unfortunately largely worn away with
only remnants remaining, is an extension of the carpet's
multicoloured silken warps, which were purposefully
arranged by the weaver to enable the creation of a colourful
decorative fringe.

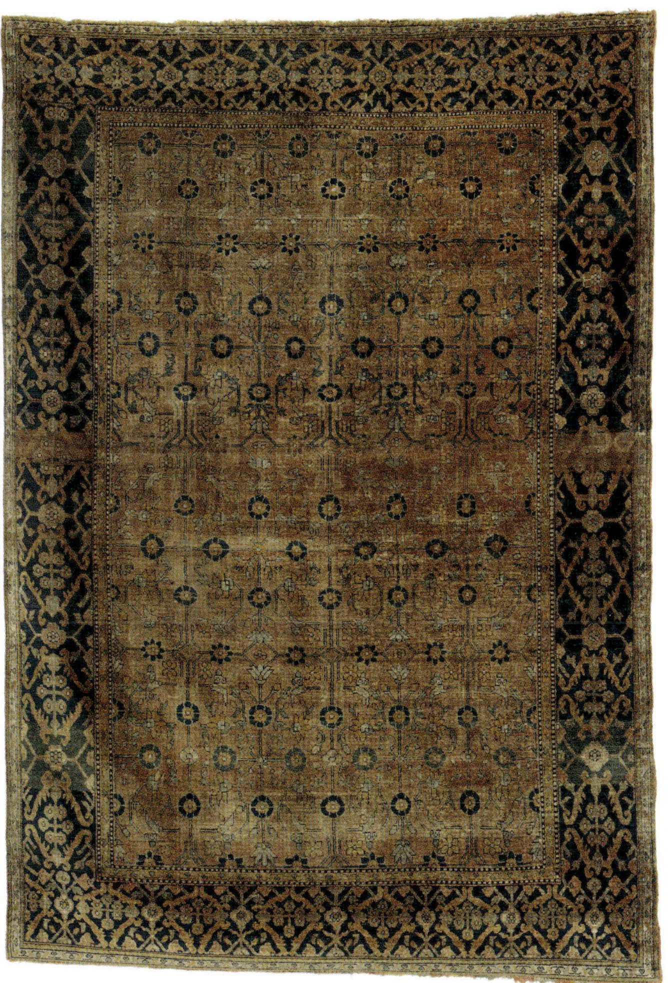

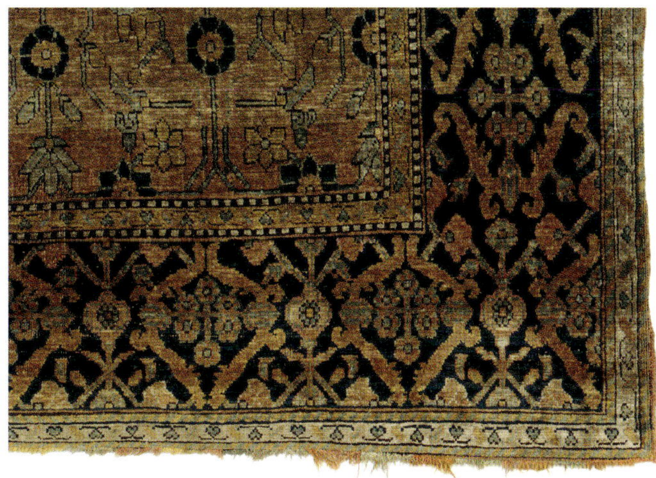

Further Reading

About the Burrell Collection

May H Beattie, 'The Burrell Collection of Oriental Rugs', *Oriental Art*, vol. 7, no. 4, 1961. Introductory article with descriptions of carpet types and assessment of significance.

Martin Bellamy and Isobel MacDonald, *William Burrell: A Collector's Life*, Glasgow Museums Publishing and Birlinn Ltd, Edinburgh, 2022. Biography of William Burrell, his life, collection and legacy.

Steven J Cohen, 'Beasts of the Imagination', *Hali Magazine*, vol. 172, summer 2012. Review article of a Burrell Collection temporary exhibition by the same name (24 March–5 June 2012), including revised expert opinion on the provenance of carpet 9.23, one of the four carpets exhibited.

Jennifer M Scarce, 'The Burrell Collection, Oriental Carpets', *Arts of Asia*, vol. 20, no. 3, May–June 1990. Introductory article presenting highlights of the Islamic carpets at the Burrell Collection, in a special issue of the journal focusing on the museum.

Islamic carpets worldwide

May H Beattie, *Carpets of Central Persia*, World of Islam Festival Publishing Company Ltd, London, 1976. Publication to accompany a major exhibition curated by Dr Beattie, exhibited in 1976 at the Mappin Art Gallery, Sheffield, and City Museum and Art Gallery, Birmingham; it includes eight Burrell Collection carpets (9.2; 9.3; 9.7; 9.10; 9.14; 9.15; 9.17; 9.120).

Steven J Cohen, 'A Fearful Symmetry, The Mughal Red-Ground "Grotesque" Carpets', in *Silk and Stone: The Art of Asia*, ed. Jill Tilden, Hali Publications Ltd, London, 1996. This chapter explores the story of the pair of carpets to which the Burrell Collection's carpet fragment 9.1 belongs.

Walter B Denny, *How to Read Islamic Carpets*, The Metropolitan Museum of Art, New York, 2014. Introductory book about pile carpets: their history, aesthetics, types and techniques.

Charles Grant Ellis, *Early Caucasian Rugs*, The Textile Museum, Washington DC, 1975. Explores the evolvement of Caucasian carpet designs, including dragon carpets.

Hali Magazine, Hali Publications Ltd, London, 1978–present. Periodical dedicated to textiles, rugs and carpets of the world, especially the Islamic world.

Leonard M Helfgott, *Ties that Bind: A Social History of the Iranian Carpet*, Smithsonian Institution Press, Washington, DC, 1994. Insightful social and historical exploration of the handwoven-carpet industry and the weaving communities in nineteenth-century Iran.

Jon Thompson, Daniel Shaffer and Pirjetta Mildh (eds), *Carpets and Textiles in the Iranian World 1400–1700*, Oxford University Press and Bruschettini Foundation for Islamic and Asian Art, Genoa, 2010. Historical exploration of early Persian carpets.

Daniel S Walker, *Flowers Underfoot: Indian Carpets of the Mughal Era*, The Metropolitan Museum of Art, New York, 1997. Explores the carpet tradition in India during the Mughal period.

Jennifer Wearden, *Oriental Carpets and their Structure: Highlights from the V&A Collection*, V&A Publishing, London, 2003. Historical comment, detailed descriptions and structural analysis, written in an accessible style.